CRITICAL ACCLAIM FOR
MICHAEL FOLEY'S POETRY

'Few poets alive are up to this sort of impertinence.'
Douglas Dunn, *Encounter*

'Pungent, witty, perceptive ... like Larkin, only sharper,
funnier and more cynical.'
Anthony Cronin, *The Irish Times*

'A remarkable writer, serious without being po-faced, making poetry ...
that can discuss the comic and trivial things central to us in a way
that's neither pretentious nor patronising.'
Robert Johnstone, *Fortnight*

'Let me lay it on the line and say with simple sincerity: Foley is fun.'
Robert Greacen, *Irish Press*

Autumn beguiles the Fatalist

MICHAEL FOLEY

BLACKSTAFF
PRESS
———
BELFAST

ACKNOWLEDGEMENTS

The Acre, The Backyards of Heaven (Scop Productions Inc., 2003), *The Black Mountain Review*, *British Council New Writing 8* (Vintage, 1999), *Cyphers*, *The Honest Ulsterman*, *The Interpreter's House*, *Leviathan Quarterly*, *Orbis Quaterly*, *The London Magazine*, *Magma*, *Metre*, *Obsessed with Pipework Quarterly*, *Paging Doctor Jazz* (Shoestring Press, 2004), *Poetry Ireland Review*, *Poetry London*, *The Poetry Review*, *The Shop*, *Smiths Knoll*, *Stand Magazine*, *The Stinging Fly*, *Thumbscrew*, *Verse*, *Writing Ulster*.

ARTS COUNCIL
of Northern Ireland

Michael Foley has asserted his right under
the Copyright, Designs and Patents Act 1988
to be identified as the author of this work.

Typeset by Carole Lynch, County Sligo, Ireland
Printed in Ireland by ColourBooks
A CIP catalogue record for this book is available
from the British Library
ISBN 0-85640-772-0

www.blackstaffpress.com

For Jane and Ryan

CONTENTS

III

THE CITIES

IV

AUTUMN BEGUILES THE FATALIST

V
THE DRUNKENNESS OF THINGS BEING CARIOUS

I

THEORIES OF
ORDER AND CHAOS

THE BUZZ

Loathing lackey moths, blundering shield bugs,
Attention-seeking butterflies, ladybirds, wasps,
I lie still in still water, know what I need
And how to take it efficiently, almost invisibly.
Only an empty thing needs to be *seen*.

For instance, this loud barbecuing buffoon
Who first builds a water effect for *my* home
Then emerges in flip-flops and shorts
To offer – at *my* feeding time – his bare flesh
(Remind me to laugh when I've laid eggs).

Crepuscule is my hour. In the magical dim
I'm an atom of twilight, a warp in the air.
Even so, I wait till he sits with his glass
Then come in low and go for calf (stealth
And precision – the smart shield and sword).

Locking onto his heat like a missile, I land
On a spacecraft's deft legs to perform keyhole
Surgery, slitting the skin with twin stylets
That vibrate like motorised carving-knife blades.
In slides the fascicle . . . seeking arterioles.

Each strike a gusher – my juices inhibit his
Bleeding inhibitor. A flow so torrential that
After the rocket technology, surgical probing
And bio-war black arts I put to shame beer guts
By drinking three times my own weight.

The blood of fools is rich and sweet,
Intoxicating. Altar wine! Ruby port!
Only adepts of excellence approach
The sublime. But even this ebriety
Disciplined – ninety seconds in and out.

Then the dark to digest this new wealth,
Draw what's needed to make cunning eggs
That can wait through a decade of drought
For a fertile fetid hour to strike. Oh yes
I walk on water . . . navigate by the moon,

Mate in mid-air at fifty feet up
And ruminate in rank pools
– But always after digestion diversion.
This evening an exquisite sunset.
I turn you my ass and shit pink.

LAFORGUE IN COBLENZ

Atrocious triple desolation – autumn . . . Sunday . . . twilight hour . . .
From the château's highest room I scan the river's far shore
– A row of villas, dirty white, and poplars stripped bare –
As the last of the shabby tourist steamers moos its way home
Defiling the mauve of the lower sky with gouts of black smoke.

And the clashing of dinner dishes, slamming of doors! The modern world
Has embarked on a conspiracy to establish that *silence does not exist*.
Though this footman's magnificent calf muscles manage a circumspect step
As he brings me innumerable delicacies – the masterworks of four chefs –
Earning barely a turn of the head (more neglected *artistes*).

Hungry only in France, I want to see, not the Rhine, but my view
Over ramshackle lumberyards next to a black canal feeding the Seine
And the billboard with a bellicose musketeer brandishing Vicat insecticide
At a luridly vatic autumn sky which predicts a tragic fate
For the woman shaking out a rug on the seventh-floor balcony opposite.

Consolations here – pale German cigarettes, Schopenhauer ('Craving
And boredom – twin poles of the human') and the hour when the English
Chapel service ends and the boarding-school girls in white dresses emerge,
Clutching leather-bound prayer books to sweetly flat chests. How hygienic
And simple and sensible they can make the degenerate world seem!

New Divine Plan – young girls from good homes will redeem fallen man.
Such is the religion of the Empress's retinue – the gaggle of permanent
Ladies-in-waiting for nobility commensurate with their evident worth.
Ardently expecting adoration, they gradually discover the truth
– That heaven neglects to ordain and a godless world does not oblige.

R for instance – fortyish but fanatically slender, with lucent white skin
(A church candle, I thought, sapling just stripped of bark),
Her blue veins prominent and long, as though to prove her blue blood,
Her enunciation careful, precise, her tone little-girl sweet
– But the eyes of a scavenging seabird, two hungry black beads.

All her intelligence and will still turn on this one weapon – sex –
Whose delicate potency wanes by the hour like a watercolour
Left out in afternoon sun. She warps and fades – but play-acts on.
Almost unused, her fine brain. We were meant to be accomplices,
I'd thought, spies like worms at the heart of the court.

Though perhaps not. *You don't care for anyone*, she informed me at last.
Truth in that. I'm the Empress's Reader and I love only books,
Those we have . . . and my own soon to come. All the time I take notes
And at night in my high room I coax brutish life into elegant form,
Blowing smoke rings at the firmament and the sterile moon.

No . . . not *books*. It's the vigil, the trance, the afflatus, the spell,
Exaltation that sweeps up the soul as supremely and strangely as ocean swell.
At such moments I know there's a shriek (blending manic elation,
Rue, irony, pain) that I – and *I alone* – can make, and sometimes
When dawn lights the fog-shrouded Rhine I indulge the mad dream:

To move to pity the indifferent stars and unsettle the granite face
Of death with a sublime late lament like the Schubert Quintet
Which makes the human vessel resonate in spite of itself,
Physically forcing you to wake and feel, to groan, quiver, grieve, keen
– As though the bows were pulled across your own aching heart strings.

WINTER IN DERRY

Not only a struggle to rise but a battle to enter St Columb's at nine.
Within the gates massed ranks of boarders with snowballs in piles.
On the pavement a huddle of dayboys in slushy soiled ice.
Out stormed the Dean, a big impatient priest, to roar in disgust:
Come in outa that! Are yese men at all? Have yese anything in yese at all?

And only the most cunning and able would ever get close to a radiator.
O Danny Boy . . . the pipes . . . the pipes . . . are . . . caw . . . aw . . . lling
– Hooky Boyle hugging warmth to taunt Danny Barr.

Fingers too numb to hold a pen, much less write.
The hot wet forests have colourful flora and enormous tree frogs with sucker feet.

Enormous boarders had purple hands. Many with circulation problems –
    in their *teens*.
Though, starving as well as frozen, they circulated rapidly and widely
    at noon:
*Mickey what's in yer sandwiches Mickey? Timata? Ah give us a half one hi give
    us a bite.*

Your tiny hand is frozen, Father O'Flaherty loved to hoot
As he straightened out numb crumpled fingers for six
And delightedly swished the strap.
Don't worry. Swing and roar: *Ah'll warm it up!*

Then returning in four o'clock twilight like hunters from taiga to hearth
    fire and home.
Throughout winter we never used slack – only lustrous top-quality coal

That burned fiercely with pulsing core reds and wild yellow and blue
  aureoles.
More resplendent than summer (Irish summer at least). Source of visions
  and dreams.
Outside all was etchings or pen-and-ink drawings but inside our heads we
  were colourists, *fauves*.

Nor did we flinch from the upper regions. Ascetic and silent as
  lighthouse-keepers,
We ascended to attics with spavined beds weighed down by heaps of
  bedclothes.
And never so luxuriant and bizarre was the buried fleshly underworld
(The heavier the stopper and deeper the pit, the weirder the animal life
  which persists).

Hooky Boyle recalling his rapture (truth or fantasy – what did it matter?):
See Mickey like Ah lie in bed an' burn me whole lad wi' the hot-water bottle.
Here a pause to make contact by hand and eye. For my concentration was
  less than total.
I know it's hard to believe now – but extravagance was *routine* then
With everywhere Mozarts of malediction, cool virtuosos of rodomontade.
An' next day Ah bust all the blisters. Fierce immobilising grip. Blazing
  visionary eyes.
Nice an' slow ye know Mickey . . . one every so often . . . unbelievable hi.

FURTHER EDUCATION

As in a Renaissance Annunciation
When a golden laser beam
Conveys the Holy Spirit down
To irradiate startled Mary's womb,
So from the one high grimy pane
A valiant ray of morning sun
Transmuted dog-eared paper heaped
On five adjacent tabletops
In the room meant for one.

But instead of radiant angels
Announcing a miraculous birth
Mild Bill Close of Admissions flapped in
On his year-round black sandals
(He had chronic feet problems)
Bearing news of the untimely death
Of the one demanding course we loved.
Shocking, the bland official words:
Projected September intake – Nil.

Immediately everyone savaged Bill
– Already denounced by outraged Joan
For the country-of-origin box on forms.
'The *real* entry criteria?' I asked Bill once.
'Only one,' he said. 'Have they a pulse?'
But Joan loved to unmask racist plots
And exhaust us with caring complaints
Like: 'We celebrate Christmas and Easter
So why not Diwali and the Chinese New Year?'

And Joe too was becalmed, unreborn
(In spite of appropriating the 'lucky' table
Two former colleagues got Poly jobs from)
But insulated by the natural blitheness of youth.
A mere course closure caused him no grief.
'We could start our own college . . . get an old
School cheap . . . these days no sweat . . . then say
Two hundred Arabs at three grand a head
— There's six hundred thousand straight off.'

Frank of course wanted to fight the decision.
A touchy, aggressive, embittered guy . . . *doomed*.
'Frank,' I said, 'you can't take *them all on*.'
In my Hollywood Mexican peasant voice:
'More men weel come . . . *men weeth guns*.'
Sore vexed Frank's soul and hungry bones.
Often I'd come in to find him hunched
Like an animal, head lowered, eyes hunted,
Wolfing his sandwiches at 10 a.m.

Ah . . . our sad sandwiches wrapped in tinfoil.
Maybe it's true that we are what we eat.
We too crushed, misshapen and limp.
Yet in sunlight the dust danced and glowed.
Accepting Bill interviewed, nodded, enrolled.
There was always further education.
Even total concentration. Whatever the subject,
The hairdressing trainees attended consistently
— Each to the hair of the one in front.

And still the Paraclete came down
To bless the piles of marked assignments
(Marks of weakness, marks of woe),
The mountains of handouts and folders of notes
('A Relational Database,' Joe used to joke),

The electric kettle, powdered milk, discoloured mugs,
The economy tin of instant coffee fine as dust
And the floor tiles – broken, missing, loose
('A health hazard!' cried Joan).

'Got the time on you?' Joe asks Frank now
And the Spirit may have touched Frank
For he suddenly looks up and around
As if for the first time overawed
By the welter and wonder of
The phenomenal world (certainly with
No urge to start on his lunch)
And almost forgetting to check his watch:
'Ten o'clock . . . *and all's well.*'

BROKEN KINGS AT NIGHTFALL

Student almost as white as his mentor
(But scarcely the wiser for all their disputing),
They sit by a bedsitter gas fire at evening,
Grey guest and his silver host, sharply declaiming:
'Who did Dante put right down with Satan?
Down in the lowest circle? *Brutus!*
Loyalty was Dante's consuming obsession.'

But grey guest, disloyal, recalls his lost love
On the day they departed for Florence at dawn,
Slew of breasts as she leaned to switch off the alarm,
Then the exquisite jolt of her bounding from bed,
Golden nimbus of glory about her head
As she drew unimpeachable white shoulders back
And insouciantly cried: 'Take a trip round *that*.'

'Did Dante ever put the wood to Beatrice?' he asks.
Silver host grunts and takes up his pipe.
'I've deplored the insistence on fealty
But perhaps his most serious error
Was to *champion vernacular eloquence*.'
Vulgar guest has to wait for the pipe to be filled.
'Dante scarcely *met* Beatrice, much less put the wood.'

Now it's Florence in summer . . . an *al fresco* dinner.
Beyond Pinot Grigio reclining in ice
(With a white napkin tastefully tied round its neck)
And above a long flowing black dress

Twilight nests in the twin holy wells
Behind the prominent clavicles
Of a beautiful woman at dusk.

'So where did he place the mean of spirit?'
'The pusillanimous and uncommitted?'
Gravely they ponder the breathing plaque.
'The emotionally crippled, yes . . . *how far down?*'
'Ah.' Silver sighs deeply and lays by his pipe.
'Only on this, the near side of the Acheron.
Only in the vestibule of Hell.'

Il Grande Caldo. Florence prostrate. Yet as they leave
The church where Dante first saw Beatrice
He finds himself unable to quell fierce desire
Or even restore the protective prepuce
Trapped behind the chafed head
And so limps along, grinning and heartsick in sun,
Staining his new leisurewear with pre-come.

Grey and Silver sequestered in reverie,
Lost in the fire's violet-streaked fulvous glow,
Gentle light touching classics in untidy stacks
On the sagging shelves, table and floor.
Abruptly comes a plangent moan.
It's the wind in the chimney behind the fire.
Apparently the sweet air is troubled tonight.

Together they harken. Silver shivers. 'And Dante
Claims that Adam and Eve had only six hours
In the garden.' Now they're terminally dumb.
Like graven images their stricken faces
Lit by the fire into which they both gaze.
Dark tobacco-smelling volumes impassively ranged.
Still tobacco smoke above like discoloured torn lace.

THEORIES OF ORDER AND CHAOS

1

A gaudy foil-wrapped Penguin will be *my* madeleine
(Or the heady scent of Pink Paraffin),
Restoring an attic room and the theories of Newton
As my mother triumphantly tiptoes in

To set down . . . on top of books . . . Royal Albert
Teacup and saucer and side plate with Penguin,
My hieroglyphs changing her pride into horror:
Sacred Heart Michael that looks very tough.

Ah then raising the eyes from the rational page
To locked-out raving wind and rain
And, an inner window shielding the heater's flame,
With sovereign ruminating pleasure exposing the bar.

2

But soon she proposed her own Grand Unified Theory
– The universe has an underlying principle: *contrariness.*
Whatever an honest soul strives to achieve
The outcome will always be just the reverse.

I should have dressed you in rags
. . . And you'd have wanted good clothes.
Should have fed you on chain bones so when you were
Handed good food you wouldn't turn up your nose.

Thus the spangled, half-nude circus girls left me cold,
My real treat the mature woman crouched in a field,
The light dying, wind swaying black trees . . . and soft
Whiteness brought down to the scandalous weeds.

3

The impenetrable mysteries of disorder and turbulence
Chaos Theory eventually came to address.
Too late for me, as it turned out. The laws
Of the old clockwork universe were deep in my bones.

Her bones being turned to dust by osteoporosis
And terminal emphysema stopping her breath,
She delivered the oldest lament: *I would do
Things all so differently if I had my time again.*

Impossible to hold back the question: *What things?*
Somehow she heaved herself upright on thin brittle arms
And from ruined lungs found enough breath to shout:
I wouldn't take so much cheek from you for a start.

REGARDING THE BED

Yet another indictment – that we scarcely see, much less thank
A partner who can *daily* and *simultaneously* meet
The two most common and pressing but mutually exclusive human needs
– At once security and adventure, support and release.

Yet a bed combines motherly warmth with the reckless *Mardi gras* of dream
In the kind of self-effacing service we never thought to see again.
Devoted, loyal and supportive all the way through life,
It will bear us up to the end, our truest four-legged friend.

In this case four short bandy ornate legs
That conceal the real grey steel legs beneath
But reveal the temperament of the former owner
Who liked to hide function with scrollwork.

Suddenly it comes to me with a shudder – *this was once my mother's bed*.
Why did I take it when I took little else?
Some unconscious dark urge to defile and avenge?
(Proust adorned a gay brothel with his dead mother's things.)

It certainly embodies her passion for furniture
And abiding dislike of the rectilinear
With its curves and curlicues and whorls,
Its flutings and spirals and frothy headboard.

Not the bed in which she died – but where her coffin was laid
While the bourgeoisie of Derry came to pay their respects,
Returning in force for the final journey
And remarking my calm with distaste (so I've heard).

Burghers, those lacking charity can often be fair.
To Derry and provincial towns everywhere
I hereby gladly give their due. You may not be
Able to live in them – *but they'll bury you in style.*

Better a solitary city death in the four-legged friend, going out
As I've lived – book in hand. My own statue – at least for a while.
Till the people next door get my first and last message – the smell.
(I too yearn for community – it's just neighbours I hate.)

Not the bed in which she died but where she spent her last days,
Dependent on massive oxygen cylinders in peeling black paint,
Grotesquely and undisguisably functional with a brass valve and gauge.
Not just giving breath, they helped anchor her withering frame to
    the earth.

As the soul becomes heavy and clinging the body lightens and craves
    release.
Every buttoned–up, shrunken, old lady now reminds me
Of my mother's last years. Those heavy coats aren't just for warmth
But to keep them from blowing away in the breeze.

And, preceding the physical, the spiritual shrinkage.
While the rites of spring fade, its old wrongs remain fresh
(My mother's sad tape loop of six ancient wrongs).
We bed down in old grievance like glad nesting birds.

After food, warmth and sex our great need is a whinge.
People gathered in caves not for safety but in order to *whinge*.
Grim and inexorable the spiritual shrinkage. Even of strong spirits
Pledged to resistance. Even of spirits not large to begin with.

Farewell ye sand dunes, laneways, sofas, back seats of cars.
All our love is now made in this bed – and at conventional hours.
Not that I'm ungrateful – not in the least.
(Ageing lovers should kneel and say grace before sex.)

But is this the only answer to shrinkage – appreciate the less more?
Is there no way to keep the small thing we are whole?
For the desiccated spirit that toughens and shrivels
Can we not find restorative unguents and chrisms?

Another function of beds – to lean on when we pray.
Sweet Lord, let not my soul be cold and hard before its flesh.
Let me marvel and praise and let nothing be stone but these tablets
   of law:
Thou shalt not shrink. Thou shalt not whinge. Thou shalt not crave.

II

THIS IS THE THING

*poems suggested by the poetry and prose
of Francis Ponge*

BREAD

From one blob of eructating soggy grey stuff
Come the mountain-range crust and soft heart of a loaf
– Not a user-friendly interface and unyielding core
But a hard shell and fragrant warm pith.

The true division of powers. But it's too soon stale.
The pith petrifies, brittle and cold, in a day,
All the interwoven flexibility and connexity gone.
Break it then and it shatters in perfumeless crumbs.

This won't wait. Cherished old friends, loved ones,
Etiologists brooding on sofas at night – even colleagues
From work (though, please God, few of these),
I now call upon all of you to break bread with me.

THE MATCH

Stalwart the long body, head hard and full
– Yet it's happy to lie in dark rows
Till the silk robes of flame give it soul.
Of course only the head can catch fire

But it needs a strong body to bear up the head
(Worthless the limp matches free from hotels)
And the contact location and style must be right
For the fruitful surprise attack, brusque, swift (a *strike*).

Harsh reality rasp . . . then a crackle and fizz
When, as though by a conjuration . . . sorcerer's art
(A suggestion of Lucifer in the sulphurous whiff),
The small neat head explodes in a halo of fire.

Though the flame's often tentative after this flare,
As if too shy to dare . . . lying low . . . guttering.
Then it catches on, bending and billowing, leaning out far
(Like the sails of a clipper exulting in wind),

Mad with joy that a uniform head,
Dark and dull, could develop
Such marvels – a pulsing blue core
And an undulating yellow and gold aureole.

Now at last it's relaxed, getting into the swing,
Strong, fulfilled, knowing how it should live
– When all of a sudden it runs out of wood,
The succulent white fuel entirely consumed.

And the worst not that this exaltation should cease
But that what's left is such a disgrace
– Brittle, ravaged and unrecognisable,
Bent as an old crone and black as a priest.

THE CANDLE

Single petal of gold on a stalk of scorched black
At the top of an alabaster column that shrinks
– This egregious bloom, flowering only at night,

Unsettles with cave shadows the contemporary gleam
Of pop-up toasters, food processors, split-level hobs.
An anachronism really – unstable and messy –

Yet it's set upon a pedestal for diners to watch.
Which they do. Oh they *do*. However gripping the talk,
Eyes will stray to and stay on the wavering gold.

Women even nurture it as though it's a living thing,
Stroking the pliant lip, staunching the hot tears,
Monitoring its equilibrium and removing its waste.

And moths of course prefer it to the fire-feigning moon
. . . Or, rather, they would if we let them in.
The strong double glazing keeps night things out.

Though now and then a shadow lurch turns us that way.
Familiar train of ragged shapes . . . the stars once more veiled.
Like the moths, meanings hover near and brush our sealed panes.

SOAP

Even manifold nature has nothing like soap.
A cold bar can seem a stone, hard, self-contained,
Withholding its essence in silent disdain
And indifferent to water's unilateral kiss
— But soap never desires the solipsism of stone.

For a start, it emits, at close range, a scent
And sequestration, though blissful, is not permanent.
Signs of stress show on soap when it's too long alone.
Its bright forehead grows dull, hardens, wrinkles, cracks up.
Though aware that involvement will grind it down,
Soap can never renege on its duty to man.

So the summons is feared — but awaited, *required*.
For as soon as it engages with water
Soap abandons its lapidary, separatist pose
And becomes lithe, elusive, fish-like, hard to hold
(No — more octopus-like. When it slithers and dives
It creates a cloud in which to hide).

For those who can manage to keep hold
(Coquetry of course in the slipperiness)
While stimulating it with water in the appropriate dose,
Soap is nothing like stone — but exults, blathers, foams,
Throws up profligate clusters of shimmering spheres,
Scented iridescent, evanescent cities of air
And makes hands lissome, supple, magnanimous, blithe,
More than glad to facilitate change so sublime
(From which, unbelievably, hands emerge *pure*).

Then if the soap is left in the water
They join in an unsolemn marriage of pleasure
For which soap does not don a gown
But the intimate garb of dalliance
– Silken kimono and harem pants.

Afterwards both are profoundly transformed.
The bar is soft, indolent, loath to emerge,
Deep in amniotic luxury, yielding its all,
Happy to perish in dissolute joy,
And the water, once limpid, is stirred up, perturbed,
Entirely suffused by a nacreous cloud,
Now so sensitive any touch makes it respond
With the lover's eternal aerostatic pretension
– To effervesce, form bubbles, take to the air.

Pastel prestidigitator! Fragrant agent of change!
(Itself willing to undergo radical change
– Marble hardness and coolness to warm mucilage)
Amphibious ingot! Susceptible pebble!
Loquacious stone ovoid! Slow-motion grenade!

Fact: though prophets would have us immersed in the Jordan
And philosophers down the deep dark well of truth,
Man may not purge himself by means of water alone
But must take his soiled hands to the humble wash bowl
With its unassuming servitor who turns none away
And is a true democrat – response always the same,
Never taking on the tone or the mark of the other
(Though from time to time it consents to wear
A mischievous monogram of pubic hair).

And was ever giving so complete?
Essence not merely proffered, involved, but *used up.*
When the service ends so might the soap.
Literally a *life of dissipation.*

Ruthless market-force Darwinists should ponder on this.
It certainly moves *me*, reluctant old stone
(I believe the banal is our natural element
But have never learned to swim in it).

Put your sweet-smelling clean hands together for soap
Which dissolves the seductive allure of the stone
Whose apparent nobility it reveals as a sham.
It is not strong but misanthropic, stingy and weak
To justify the refusal to give by refusing to take.

THE SPIDER

Each day it fashions (in less than an hour)
Twenty metres of what looks like frail gossamer
But can stretch to ten times its own length and not break
(Nor yet recoil too rapidly and throw the catch off).

Baffling even the start. Does it fling out a line?
Abseil down without losing the thread?
Then the simultaneity of the spinning and weaving
(But never embroidering – webs are for *use*).

Every freshly spun, silken line, weightless but strong,
Is precisely set out in a filigree pattern
The maker can never step back from to scan
– Yet with which it is never too closely involved.

So many get snared in their own cunning mesh
But the spider skips free on eight scandalous legs
To perform jump jet take-offs, vertiginous sky dives,
Long tightrope walks (some at *sprint* speed . . . *upside down*).

Such entelechy – effortless, blithe –
Both deflates and incites. What ineffable joy
If *we* could hurl ourselves fearlessly into the void
And weave astonishing filaments above the abyss!

It looks so easy when you see it done.
Just throw out a few supple but strong sentences
That will bear your full weight if you're nimble and light
And provide a sound base for the encompassing net.

What is glory but luring the world to a web
Which the innocent flutterers can't even see
– Much less the dark engineer lying in wait
(Now religiously still) to rush out

In mad glee and fling itself on the prey,
Immobilise the flailing with a surgical strike
Then wrap it in cling film to see the light
(And preserve it moist and fresh for lunch).

Oh then substanceless, thoughtless ones
– Flies, midges, moths – those who whirr, buzz
And drone in the hither and thither of hectic
Flight paths, reassured by the swarm,

Will have time as they quiver in the indifferent wind
Contemplating the motionless brooding Black Prince
To rue the meaninglessness of their movement and noise
And learn . . . too late . . . that stillness and silence are wise.

THE WASP

The wasp seems to have adopted on a permanent basis
The derangement and frenzy of flies in a crisis
(e.g. zapped by fly spray or stuck to fly paper).
No, it's even more crazy – hyperactive, inordinate, raging,
The twin antennae always flailing, ponderous abdomen oscillating,
Both its pairs of wings restlessly whirring even on a tabletop walk.

And its constant intimidating sizzle
– Like electrical equipment that's developed a fault
Or a searing hot Balti dish straight from high flame.

Only crushing it to pulp makes it calm.
For cut it in two and the halves will still jive
Like a pair of adolescents at an all-night rave.
If anything, the movement more frenetic and wild.
Too demented to notice its own demise.

Garish colours, provocative hovering, noise
– As with chauvinists of once-powerful now minor states
Who perpetually seethe with rage and hate,
Determine to give and take only offence,
Flaunt insignia, swarm in dark nests . . . adore beer.

Other wasp passions: Coke, sugared food
. . . And the honey it can't itself produce.
(Hence a fascinating seminar topic:
Has Anger Always a Sweet Tooth?)

Most revealing is its love–hate relationship with fruit.
It loathes but haunts lusciousness, ripening,
The satori of developing in silence and peace,
That maturity and serenity it can never achieve.

Observe a wasp root in the juicy softness
With a gleaming metallic proboscis,
Hairy thorax and maleficent abdomen throbbing.
This is not nourishment but pillage and rape.
It intends to despoil and contaminate.
(Birds attack too but don't leave poisoned wounds.
They would never use chemical weapons on fruit.)

Triumphant, it lifts blank obsidian eyes
And four bright yellow daubs on a mask of high gloss.
Aggression loves sun colours rampant on black.
The sun is implacable, fierce, absolute.
But even the hottest of summers grows cool.
Then the wasp is confused – at its most dangerous.
Any contact at all and its sting lashes out.

As though it can sense that its days are few,
That it missed the unique assignation with beauty
And its buzzings and blazons are not signs of strength
(You don't have to pretend to be what you are)
But reveal to the world as it briefly sidesteps
Only isolation, emptiness, inadequacy and fear.

MOLLUSCA

When Nature declines to give essence a form
And replaces the skeleton with a holding wall
We're tempted to think of paste in tubes
And interpret the attitude as scorn.

But what scorn would fashion a reliquary deft as an inlaid jewellery case,
Use a transcendental geometry for the exquisite shape
(The connecting lines of successive whorls are often spiral helices)
And put the most effulgent beauty on the *inside* face?

The creature without a defining matrix is not a despicable gob of phlegm
But often a sensitive principled soul in need of protection from the world
(Molluscans abhor real estate and the hideous concept of 'starter homes'.
Content, grateful, modest, their last home's their first.)

Sequestration and sustenance – these are the needs.
Like ourselves with our through lounges, books and CDs
(Though how handy to backpack your home and withdraw when
    you please
– A great boon in committees and brainstorming teams).

For the human essence too is a formless, quivering, fearful thing
– The terrible secret Man needs to conceal.
Hence the fetish for armature – muscles like steel
And our steel-girdered towers of incommensurate size.

Disinclined to admire the Pharaohs for employing a multitude to
    commemorate one
(And anyone else who achieves their effects by bawling into a megaphone),

I reserve my praise for monkish scribes who secrete their
    monuments alone
And are spurred by obligation only, not celebrity or gold.

Ineluctably formed by the living process
Like sexual fluid, tears and sweat,
Words are a *natural* exudate,
The grey ooze that forms the astonishing shell.

A field trip – to the patio to look at a snail.
Self-possessed, singular, dandyish, cool,
He has no need of family or networking friends.
To Nature alone his allegiance is pledged.

His entire body kisses the nurturing earth
While his sensitive horns salute the sky
But retract at a hint of abuse or attack
(Self-sufficiency alas is often hated and feared).

Safely tucked in, he cunningly goes where he's kicked
And confirms his superior wisdom by wintering out in a hypogeum,
Shell interred, body curled in and entrance closed off
With a beautifully whorled, shining seal like a varnished pine knot.

Only in spring may we see once again
His nobility, stateliness, style, acumen.
What happiness and joy to be such an enlightened citizen
Of the independent state of Mollusca and its elegant capital Gastropod.

Such a pleasure to see him move out at full stretch
In the rain-renewed world he loves, fragrant, lush, bright,
Spiral shell now a fashion accessory cocked to one side,
Proud antennae alert and lithe. Note the two sets.

A front pair comb the ground, the back two scan the sky
(His eyes are forever out on stalks)
In a parallel probe that puts poets to shame,
Transcendent and down-to-earth — *both at the same time.*

Is not this the ideal way to proceed
— At a sinuous, measured, methodical pace,
Voluptuously undulant as classic Matisse
And never distracted by greed or caprice?

In the rear an impressively regal long train,
A bright trail like a jet track or ship's silver wake
Which, as much as his carriage, consoles and inspires.
If only until the next downpour, our drivel can *shine.*

THE HORSE

Moderately exceeding us in girth and height, the horse has magnificent round eyes
(Though its lids are half-closed), flaring nostrils, ears always pricked up, a long muscular neck.

The finest of man's domestic creatures and truly his designated mount.
Absurd and lost on top of an elephant, man is appropriately enthroned on a horse.

But if horses no longer have a function in cities, do we have to abandon them to zoos?

Not entirely! At times . . . like a haunting . . . a dream . . .
The resonant clack of hoofs on tarmac falls on impoverished city ears.
Immediately I rush to the window. A policeman goes by on a magnificent bay
Which even in a somnolent side street
Shudders and lunges and skitters sideways and has to be pulled back straight.

Sensitive to the very tip of every extremity,
His lustrous and constantly rippling flanks have the beauty and richness of period furniture,
Gleaming well-preserved ebony or mahogany
. . . But are not made to endure the importunate flies.
He snorts, tosses his head, his hoofs hammer the road.

Pelt on fire, as I've said . . . but with a restlessness so deep that the bones
   of his skeleton must feel like pebbles in the path of a tumultuous
   mountain stream.

Continually trembling on the edges of frenzy,
Impatience bursts out of his nostrils which act as exhausts to vent the fumes
That would otherwise mount to the brain and make him whinny, rear
   and bolt.

The world is apparently too much with him. Everything impinges and
   overwhelms.
Hypersensitive nose and ears . . . ultrasensitive eyes.
(Perhaps the most beautiful tribute we pay him is to blinker his eyes.)

Just a beast – but refined, finicky, neurasthenic as Proust.

Fastidious gourmet of grass and air and hence a producer of straw
   brioches and fragrant, thunderous farts.

What am I saying – *gourmet* of air? He gets intoxicated, high on the stuff.
Air's illicit, addictive, sublime. Every breath is like solvent abuse.
Hence he plunges his head into air, shakes his mane at air, kicks up his
   hind legs at air.
I think he would like to *take to* the air,
Inspired by the passage of the turbulent clouds
To which he pledges undying allegiance by prancing and stamping the
   hateful ground.

But why do the forces of law and order use this prince of unrestraint?
Because latent frenzy is sensed by the rider – and the crowd the rider
   must control.
Mounted, who would not surrender to the atavistic urge
To lead a heady charge, hunt down and wantonly skewer
The pitiful cowering foot soldiers of life?

Yet the horse itself has no weapons
(Other than biting, kicking, bucking).
Hence the urge to give it something
And propose an armed model – the unicorn.

But legendary even without a horn
Is my bay horse seen at close range later
Penned in his stall behind the station,
Where I bring my daughter for ancient magic
(Courtesy of the new-style community policing).

Contemporary the elegant legs in stilettos and the smackable trim high-set
  chorus-girl's ass
But medieval and disturbingly potent the mingled odours of leather and
  dung,
Like a pungent aromatic omelette from the eggs of the goose that lays
  golden eggs
Though resembling economy-size rum truffles flavoured with rum from
  between the legs
(Why do the droppings of cats and dogs never enchant us?
Tubular, paste-like and vilely adhesive, they too much resemble human
  waste).

Noble horse! Great saint! Anonymous humble monk at prayer in the
  shadowy depths of a bare cell.

Did I say *monk*? It's *pope* I mean, pope on a palanquin of golden excrement,
A peek-a-boo pontiff who shows to all comers a blossoming heart-shaped
  behind
On a pair of trembling legs that terminate in nifty high-heeled ankle
  boots.

BEAUTIFUL SLEEK RUMP IN A STABLE
HORSE OR HERO OR GREAT SAINT?

A PONTIFF AT PRAYER?
OR A SCHOOLBOY DETAINED?

WHY THE JINGLING OF CHAINS?
HEAVY THUDS IN THE STALL?

TELL ME WHAT IT ALL MEANS
WHAT GOES ON IN THERE?

Modern heresy . . . thinking and questions instead of awe.

Disturbed in whatever rite, he turns on us his sacerdotal eyes . . .

BIRDS

Always taken off-guard by the suddenness and violent caprice of their flight
(Both the arrow and bow, catapult and projectile in one)
And the spread of the immediately extended wingspan,
We have barely a moment to regain our composure
When we're stunned by the economy of their folded repose
– Like a well-designed bijou bedsitter where the bed retracts into the wall
Or a Swiss army knife with all its gadgets concealed.

But in decor deluxe. So completely upholstered nothing structural shows
And you would have to probe deep to locate joints and bones – to
    establish where flesh is and where it is not,
Feel the skeleton, delicate, fragile, remarkably small for the overall size,
Little more than a matchstick-frail cage you could crush with one squeeze
(The fish skeleton even more light – but not a crushable sphere and
    incomparably better protected by flesh).

Just illusory security in the panoply of feathers – like a child with its own
    comfort-blanket built in
Or an adult with a permanent duvet and pillow of down
(Ideal for the harassed executive at moments of stress).

But none of this communicates the *essence* of birdness. What does it feel
    like to *be* a bird?
Imagine yourself as an armless creature with flipper feet and spindly legs
Obliged to hop instead of walk, run a predator-sensor in the back of your
    head
(Though the mobile neck is a help with this) and extend the same
    greeting to all comers – *flight*.

This intractable shyness, the Mozartean elegance of their swift arabesques,
their wide-eyed and delicate, highly strung uselessness, their delightful
trills and little cries
– It's all very Regency, very *refined* (and thus perfect for dinner mats and
good Christmas cards)
But remember the realities of period artifice.
The adorable darlings are smelly and lousy, with soiled collars, matted
wigs, dusty torn ruffs
(And their principal in-flight entertainment is dropping Number Two on us).

Nevertheless, we continue to look up. If not for the wingbeat of the
Andean condor
Then the swallows' vertiginous veering and banking in disciplined wingtip
formation,
Their impassioned and vivid calligraphy on the pastel vellum of twilight
air,
Or the perfect control and poise of the lone gull sweeping low over the
waters – like a swooning glissando by Johnny Hodges.

The ecstatic flight of any bird is like the signature of God.
And don't we see the Holy Spirit in the form of a dove?

So why do we loathe the dove's cousins, the birds that share our cities –
pigeons?
Don't they let us come closer than other birds do? Don't they offer
enchantment on squalid streets daily?
Aren't they tasteful enough in their fat rainbow ruffs blending, oil-sheen-
like, bottle green, burgundy, dark brown and grey,
The colours of the socks and scarves given at Christmas to family men
beyond reproach?

Unhappy pigeons, you're too much like us. When we look we see only
ourselves,
Our own cauterised indifference and fretful herd boredom, the
squandered elation we can never regain.

Long forgotten their cliffs, crags and caves, the seigneurial flourish in
    extravagant air.
Goaded to take off, they flap up a little . . . then sink back a few metres
    further away.
Now nothing holds their attention – not even the rubbish they think they
    crave. They rush and peck . . . and move on
And are seldom alone or even in couples, preferring the company of the
    comforting throng.

Haunting fear – that our dullness is final. We detest them because they
    remind us
That there is a tide in the affairs of men which taken at the flood etcetera
But also a moment of petrifaction when the hardening reaches a
    critical mass,
A moment that can never be identified, much less undone
– One evasion, one dismissal, one wisecrack too many
And immediately a life is set forever in stone.

STONES

So the blazing globe cooled, leaving fire to the sun
And when grandeur was dead life was born
(A reminder that these two will never be one
And that counsellors need to talk on).

Now the petrified rock forms are temple and tomb
To the radiant fire king who once was the world
And like unemployed losers too lazy to shave,
Withdraw into mutism, let growth invade

With a cracked grin at blooms in pinks barely more bright
Palest copies of pale sunset skies
Which themselves are faint ghosts of primordial fire
When rocks blazed through the firmament haloed in flame.

Though great blocks are still moved by the bulldozer sea
Which hugs, caresses, dandles, kneads
(One shapeless grey monster embracing another)
Till, broken down, each piece is polished and smooth.

Then they're coddled like sugared almonds in the depths of the mouth
And only spat out for the fun of the noise
When they're pitched with a roar on the sloping beach
(But, in case further sucking's required, within reach).

Thus there's no lost ancestral stone race.
Craggy mammoths, bright boiled sweets and dust coexist
As on this Irish beach where, below broken cliffs
And above fine grey sand, beach stones form a piled line.

Very symbol of all that endures undefiled?
No – in nature that endlessly fades and revives
Only stone truly dies (which wind makes
You recall by blowing sand in your eyes).

In every way halfway between cliff and sand
These beach stones are reconciled – mortal but calm.
Too mature to claim victimhood for trauma at sea,
They understand that travail was their finishing school.

Where the dirt-clotted, jagged-edged hill stones would cut,
These are content to be lifted up,
Self-contained, sleekly rounded, delightfully whorled,
Unpossessable Buddhas of the natural world.

Unlike grovelling gravel, too large to walk on.
Unlike untravelled land stones, too rounded for walls.
Apparently lacking attachment – yet strong
(Winds that fell trees can't budge one of these).

Nor are they even slaves to water though the sea may claim them back.
Since their smoothness is crucial it's sea that serves *them*.
Through its chaos and fury they roll unperturbed,
Much reduced but unchanged – homomorphs of themselves.

No sooner away from the water than dry
And even when finally ground to sand
The sea flushes through without leaving a trace
(Never that collaborator's ignominy – mud).

To the vanquished quest heroes who wander here,
Ground down by years, lacking stature and fire,
Not the posturing sea but the stones of the beach
Cold, diminished, too many – teach honour and grace.

III

THE CITIES

LONDON PASTORAL

It's a dim, sequestered, mongrel street
Where stretches of peeling terrace and moribund businesses alternate.
First some homes . . . then an ancient Greek café where
Three ancient Greeks play a card game with resolute backs
To a flickering black-and-white television high on a wall.

Next the sightless grey of *W Rees (Spectacle Frames)*
And a junk shop seeking 'Deceased Effects', which produces this effect itself.
Though *Enco Products (London)* has a colourful shelf
Showing Callaloo, Fruit A Pain, Dunn's River Pigeon and Gungo Peas
And a can of BIG BAMBOO JAMAICAN IRISH MOSS VANILLA DRINK.

Jamaican Irish Moss? But there is no time to think
For here is LS *Orthopaedics* with a lifeless rubber plant
And a grinning, bald, middle-aged man in commodious corset
And underpants, his right hand nonchalantly held behind his back
While his left bears aloft the sign: CAMP POSTURE BELTS.

No business could top *that* – so more dingy curtains,
Stained doors flanked by bells bearing rain-blurred names,
Cracked concrete front gardens with shrouded bikes, weeds
And black bins next to steps down to barred basement flats
. . . Even buddleia sprouting from eaves. Timeless peace!

And now a burnish of benediction lights the foggy, scored face
Of the shackled gum dispenser by *The Daily Needs Store*.
Where without haste the heaped refuse sacks
Learn mutually accommodating shapes,
Plastic crates are peed on by a calm spotted dog.

L'INCONNUE

Diurnal throne of voluptuousness – a Piccadilly Line seat.
Woman doing her lips, frowning violinist fingering chords on his case,
Two agape Asian youths with connected heads (shared Walkman leads),
Headscarfed gypsy soliciting mutely beneath a lord stabbed in the back
(Murder Mystery Dinner Theatre – 3 courses, 3 murders, DJ till late).

Then the joy of a fortyish *inconnue* rejecting bestsellers for *Scarlet and Black*.
She could be Madame Renan in fact, the selfless mother with an
    ardent heart.
Profound, sensitive, lucent, maternal eyes. Compassion, tolerance,
    tenderness.
Certainly if you had a little accident she wouldn't get cross.
Alas she alights at her station. Follow in radiant vasselage? No.

The glory of love for the *inconnue* is that it is love at last sight.
Besides, a sign has been granted me. My mysterious ministry is to listen
    and watch,
To observe, consider, speculate – which is solidarity of a sort.
The heavy doors shudder shut. With a sigh and a tremble we gather
    momentum.
Equally hazardous, rich and strange – the journey into the known.

JARDIN DU LUXEMBOURG

Not a trace of blue – but such a symphony of grey.
Authentic shades of Doisneau, Brassaï,

Granite, brains, old movies, truth . . . and noble Penguin
Modern Classics (till they turned lime green).

The air astringent, cool, austere,
Packed with gooseberry notes like a well-chilled Sancerre,

Adversarial wind spoiling French symmetries,
Discomposing the manicured uniform trees,

Blowing poised fountain jets to undignified shreds
And raising on straight gravel paths twister clouds.

Hail, violator of air space and territorial waters,
Exuberant wrecker of Irish comb-overs,

Unresting and keen as the mind of God,
Eternal inquisitor of the trammelled world!

No wonder Cioran came here every day
To wander and hone his exemplary

Apothegms ('Let us prevent at any price
Those with clear consciences from living in peace').

Even the heavy old men playing chess
Look like poets in exile nourished by loss.

Everyone else a philosopher or adulterer
. . . And probably both. *I'm* here

With an interesting older married woman of course.
Won't recall till we're home she's *my* spouse.

She too transfigured by Paris,
Alert and radiant and mischievous,

Not just a joy to look on
But tangy and zestful as *tarte au citron*

– A far cry from these soft nymphs who swoon
On the busts (even round gay Verlaine)

Though at least they gave Flaubert (the bourgeois-despiser
Who liked a touch of bitterness to season his pleasure)

A plain, nymph-free stone bench
– Which today has a stinking *clochard* at full stretch.

Divine piquancies open and rouse the sealed heart.
(Though my tooth has grown long, let it never be sweet.)

Gustave, you might have been less disabused
If you'd known that the pH range of cooze

Is 3.8 to 4.5 – just a tinch more
Acidic than *café noir*

But (the proof that God's in Heaven)
Less bitter than lemon.

RUE DE MALTE

Urban frenzy never penetrates this narrow street
Where facing blocks of seven storeys make a crevice dark and deep.
Any fearful little insect would be cosy in here.

Also immensely reassuring – age, decay and disrepair,
The stained façades and crumbling courtyards glimpsed behind
    battered doors.
Time which cuts down blithely gorgeous may not notice drab and dour.

A worker in overalls leans contentedly on the bar of Café des Sports.
At a leisurely pace the Moroccan grocer builds a front-of-shop stall.
Outside the *charcuterie* a woman writes on the board.

In the gutter cleansing and cooling waters tranquilly course
And a corpulent pigeon waddles across the road to bathe dirty feet.
Could marginality and dilapidation be prerequisites of peace?

On the corner three African street-cleaners dressed in bright green
Lean together on long brooms and gravely confer:
The Wise Kings calmly considering options after their star has
    disappeared.

CANAL SAINT-MARTIN

It commences on the Seine but shrewdly goes underground *tout de suite*
To avoid the boulevards and tourist scene and re-emerge olive green
In the little-frequented area north of the Place de la République.
Here high-arched old footbridges span tranquil quays
And cobbles, gas lamps, weathered grey stone, plane trees and cast iron
Create the illusion of escape from time.

But even in mid-August leaves dot the water
Which a sudden delinquent gust now idly scores
– Like a finger drawn swiftly across velvet pile –
And a sudden loud thud makes the rapt dreamer start.
Falling along with leaves – chunks of tree bark.
Perhaps these old waterways should still do light work.

So here comes the barge *Jackie* at a leisurely pace
As befits a man-and-wife crew in late middle age,
He in the bows staring grimly ahead
And she at the back of the stern looking back.
Even a long boat is not long enough
To accommodate the *longueurs* of long married love.

Café le Pont Tournant provides a perfect vantage point
For observing the bridge turn to let *Jackie* pass.
A loutish youth calls to an older man cutting his bread
With a pocket knife – and the knife is obligingly thrown across
For comparison, comment . . . *dispute*. Grey head springs to his feet.
Enchantment zone fury! A knife fight! No – arm-wrestling bout.

Youth immediately begins to prevail – so Age declares
A false start. Is permitted this cheating . . .
Then does it *again* (the apparent lout in fact benign)
And without warning grabs the slack arm, slams it down,
Shouts, goes into a victory dance, gazes smugly around.
Avert, oh *avert*, the eyes from this disgrace to grey hair.

Whereupon, with a shackled god's roar, the bridge
Goes into its turn. Suddenly still waters gush.
Frightened pigeons fly up. Not estranged after all,
The exemplary *Jackie* couple work together, share a joke.
And across the cabin roof – prickly, tough but green with love,
A row of tiny cacti in carefully hand-painted pots.

After this the canal takes a gentle turn east
To a long stretch entirely deserted except for morose fishermen.
They never catch a thing – and least of all a human eye.
Equally blank and grim the grey façades along here.
Then Institut Supérieur d'Études Comptables et Financières,
Austere – but disquieting. How did *accountants* get into the zone?

Which ends at La Villette with flashing steel and mirror glass.
Those who would cleave to enchantment must cross
To the opposite quay and return. The road bridge here
Operates vertically – and already the road is closed.
Yet the high footbridge next to it never gets used.
Mature wayfarers wait by the barrier, held by the spell.

Nothing nearer the eternal than a torpid canal.
Who remains by these waters shall always be blessed,
Never yield to embitterment, hanker or fret.
For amid such variety who could grow bored?
Pigeons wander grey stone. Olive green cradles clouds.
One old iron bridge revolves – the other moves up and down.

CIMETIÈRE DU PÈRE-LACHAISE

Paris is radiant. Sunlight exults in bare flesh
– But not ours. It's time, *hélas,* to cover up
These flabby arms, red–vein–splotched legs.
Though we manage a brisk enough clip

On the steepening Rue de la Roquette
. . . And even climb it hand in hand.
We may be mutton dressed as mutton
But go to the slaughter like lambs.

Or, in this case, Père-Lachaise – to commune
With Abélard and Héloïse . . . whom we can't seem to find.
Searching for illegible moss-covered stone, we forget
That long-term partners always leave the starter home.

Well away from the crowded terraces, the tomb of 1817
Has dark supine figures, mock-classical pillars,
Lavish grounds with tidy gravel, tall railings all round
But is vulgar and dismal rather than grand.

And for poor Abélard no respite.
Separated from his girl and his nuts while alive,
He is now forced to lie through eternity
With a hideous Walt Disney dog at his feet.

They get more flowers, though, than the cultural great.
(Plus a packet of condoms today, witty touch.)
All the world loves a lover? Not quite.
The world will love only an *unfulfilled* lover.

For who would remember had Abe kept his knackers
And jazzed Ellie weekly for forty-odd years,
Twice a week on good weeks, every day
On their rare breaks away from the kids?

Lovers who wish to be commemorated have to part or die young.
Better to rot unsung. Though I like the Merina tribe's Memorial Day
When they dig up their loved ones and douse them with booze.
A rite the Irish should adopt (the living also get a drop).

This additional stage should be introduced
– Lay each on his love for twenty minutes or so
(But an hour for the tender old. Not even Death
Should cramp foreplay and afterglow).

I have come to understand the need for ritual at last.
We who are going nowhere must commemorate ourselves.
Invent our own profane rites . . . elevate . . . *solemnise.*
Hence the ceremony of the aperitif . . . and pre-aperitif.

Every morning I take sparkling wine (*brut* of course,
Never sweet) from a dusty shelf in Monoprix
And conceal it in the deli fridge behind the Vignotte.
By evening it's cold as Flaubert's heart

And I bring it to our top-floor hotel room, cramped and dim
But illuminated by a hierophant in a long flowing dress,
The two specially bought glasses ritually cleansed
(No disposable vessels – nor would teacups suffice).

At once wild and serene, the strange glory of evening
May match that of noon. The day ripens slowly.
No trumpery mars the last rest of De Nerval, Apollinaire,
Bizet, Corot. The plainest of black slabs for Proust.

As deep turquoise lesions of late light
Emblazon the sky in the west we climb on
Past more tiers of illustrious dead to discover
The unknown but numinous Léopold Fucker (1901–1985)

Where we pause for breath and wild surmise
(A Madame Fucker? Little Fuckers?)
Humbled afresh by the glorious mystery:
Everything passes – but splendour abides.

PASSAGE D'ENFER

A long row of identical
Blank grey façades.
Not a sinner about.
Cobbled street with no cars.

Pent and brooding – but calm.
It was sure you would come.
So push a door – any door –
And mount the narrow dim stair,

The musty smell familiar
Though you can't say from where.
Here's the big first-floor room
With a high ceiling covered

In damp stains and cracks
– A lost continent you seem
To have often explored.
And how knowingly

It gleams in the corner,
Your illuminist adept
– A full-length framed mirror
Growing secret dark blooms.

ETERNAL YOUTH AND TASTI D-LITE

1

Afoot with my vision, in a manner of speaking – gauche and rapt in a
    yellow cab – I'm
Admonished by a house side in Brooklyn: *Is it nothing to you, all ye that
    pass by?*
And cry, *I'm electrified only by everything.* Even the numbers and letters are
    resonant
. . . Taking the A train to West 22nd Street. Everywhere Tasti D-Lite. And
    the quantities.
Not just meals, *toilet bowls* bigger . . . and more full of water. Every cup
    runneth over
And is filled again free. If I had time for sex, my ejaculate would be
    kingsize. America,
I am reconciled even to baseball hats and peevish dogs carried in padded
    bags . . . but
Not to the flags. Hotdog stands flying flags? Here more of everything . . .
    except silence,
Irony, cemeteries. How could the city that never sleeps die? It won't even
    age. *Wrinkle*
*Fill, Buttock Implants, Eyelid Surgery, 24hr Gym (My Personal Trainer won't
    buy tired*
Excuses). Even while talking they jog in place. And mothers with
    pushchairs fanatically
Jogging. In eternal youth's flushed sweating solipsism, blindly the joggers
    pound by.

2

It is certainly a privilege to see so much confusion – though Miss Moore
may not have

Appreciated the muttering bum who drags a supermarket trolley full of
empty beer cans

Past The Rising Dragon Tattoo and Body Piercing Parlour where a young
girl takes off

Her blouse to offer a flawless back. No! Don't cross blind and get knocked
down

At Señor Swanky's Mexican Café and Celebrity Hangout by a yellow cab
advertising

Flashdancers Gentlemen's Lap-Dancing Club. When you still haven't even
begun the Met.

Four Caravaggios . . . *five* Vermeers. Hot Caravaggio would have loved all
of this.

He'd be tattooed and pierced – and even cool Vermeer might have been
figuratively pierced.

Inscrutable Hopper did love it of course. Here's the house where for
thirty-four years

He hauled coal up four flights, painted, fought with his wife. Unmarked –
house, I mean.

You would have to mark every house. So many seekers and even now
such possibility.

A squirrel skips niftily over Fifth Avenue. Here even shy woodland
creatures may thrive.

CITIES OF THE SOUTH

Cities of the sensual south, I love your squalor, heat and smells,
The tranquil necrosis of buildings and elders, decay understood
And accepted – plus, a greater marvel even than your antiquities,
The nine-year-old piano accordionist in new trainers playing 'My Way'
. . . And the nimbleness and ingenuity of your adolescent pickpockets,
Necessitating a money belt . . . clammy and itchy. Away with it at last
In late afternoon for companionable sex in the sun-blazoned room.
Then the redolent night. Out to follow the scent of blocked drains
Down an alley to a little square where children play, old men nurse
Bellies on benches, old women in black sit by doors on hard chairs
And the dead coloured bulbs of some festival sway between trees
Where a table waits – paper cloth, cheap glasses, jug of house red.

AN OLD BAR IN MADRID

The *madrileño* waiters are stocky and small
But their *ginebras con tónica* are slender and tall
And delivered with splendid abandon, the bottle
Not only upended but pumped down as well
(With the free hand usually balancing a full tray of drinks)
So the gin cascades over stacked ice . . . welcome sight . . .
For it's crowded and noisy and smelly and hot
Where five of the seven ages of man share the same small bar
And all drink and snack, smoke, talk at once and throw
Oil-sodden serviettes, olive stones, toothpicks and butts
On the floor. Next to tattoos and T-shirts
Are old men with fancy canes, women with fans.
Even those with no teeth are dressed up to the nines.
Nor do years cow the middle-aged pair who now fierily kiss
And squeeze each other's behinds – she, an overweight Carmen
With lime green stretch pants and long, badly dyed hair,
He, a little bald man in a cream suit, pink shirt and tie,
Black patent shoes. Short and fat – but a peacock – he pirouettes,
Snaps out his cuffs, holds aloft like a matador's sword his cigar
. . . Then resumes feeling Carmen's bum. Suddenly song!
Not a record or drunk. A songbird. But where? *Where?*
Out across from the door, above the balcony
Cradling a bicycle and the next with an upside-down sink,
Someone's put out a caged bird which lustily sings,
Its bright thrown-back head leading the eye up and up
Many floors further up to the final surprise
– Leaning out from the tenement roof at its corner,
A shanty of tarred boards beside the full moon.

ANOTHER REALM OF THE FALLEN FROM GRACE
Calle Atocha

Eccentric as ours, a creator who splices a pet shop and jeweller's
So bracelets and necklaces sit beside ferrets, toads, scorpions, beetles,
Iguanas with heads carved from granite and bodies of faded brocade.

No wonder the tropical fish look disgusted – sublime but confined
Among ornaments – Underseas Action Adventure Scenes – cruise liner
Picturesquely broken in two, diver tying a chain on an old treasure chest.

Here's a case with a cock-and-balls joke candle next to the suffering Christ.
A camp Saint Sebastian rolls his eyes: *More arrows!* Mad but engaging,
The white rat agrees, with a sudden burst of running on its wheel.

There's even a serpent – a shabby old boa, face pressed to its glass
Straining up at the flitting and tweeting – oblivious, constant – suspended
Above in a cage of improbably multi-coloured thumbsize songbirds.

EARLY MORNING IN ROME

It's early morning on the first day in Rome where so many have come
But are now dead and gone — whereas this late invader in leisurewear
And unbarbaric, newly trimmed nostril hair is *here* . . . his head clear
Though heady with imminence, Factor Fifteen on his sensitive
    countenance
And his sensibly Clarks-shod feet ready to march on the legion
Of Caravaggios in *palazzi* and churches . . . even out on the streets.
Wasn't this drunk, directing the traffic, in *The Flagellation of Christ*?
The entire Eternal City thrums with the tension of getting to work
But this pilgrim's so light he could levitate, soar above these weathered
Umber and salmon-pink buildings whose impertinent TV dishes vie
With the cupolas. There's even the sanction of augury — that most
    propitious
Of omens from entrails, a substantial dump just before leaving the hotel.

UNEASEFUL DEATH

1

Outside the station the sleeping drunk's sprawled by a shirtless hunchback
Sitting passive and mute – but the proactive one-legged beggar springs up
And propels himself after me waving his knee stump and crying *Signore!*
Then a loitering trio of bag-eyeing toughs . . . and a wide roaring road
Before silently, smoothly, an automatic metal gate swings to admit me
To order, good taste and serenity. It's the Protestant Cemetery with elegant
Cypresses, clipped hedges, mown grass . . . and the shock of clear
   signposting
In a disorganised city. Shelley is straight ahead, Keats to the left. So left
For the bleak stone: '. . . who on his Death Bed in the Bitterness of his
   heart . . .'
The tireless foe, bitterness, claimed even Keats. Death was not as easeful
In reality as in poesy. When, as though to remind that the easeful thing's
   life,
My leg's nudged by soft warmth – a purring black cat with occult yellow
   eyes.

2

And now I notice the others – stretched out as though they own the
   place
. . . On the paths . . . under trees . . . One cool voluptuary lolls on the
   grave
Of Duchessa Maria Regina Castello di Carcaci (née Maunders-Drake).
Such cunning cats to find the haunt of brute-loving Brits – Edwin
   Archibald,

Emma Maud Whybrow, Isabel Huntly Lenox Hodgkinson, Ambrose Lace
Of Little Woolton (but who let in Jim Dolen, Actor, 'now starring in
    Eternity'?).
There's even a donation box marked: 'For the Cats'. And explanatory
    leaflets
On 'The Guardians of the Departed': 'These little friends provide loyal
Companionship for the deceased.' It's enough to make a cat laugh.
The black leg-rubber eyes me with scorn. Careful, puss! You're half-wrong
On this one. My head may have converted to Protestantism but my heart
Is still a medieval Catholic . . . a mad, greedy, murderous Emperor-Pope.

3

And lying once more by Keats but now at peace, Severn, young too at the
    time
But required to do everything – worn out from sleeplessness, nursing,
    chores,
Fears – dwindling money cut off at the bank while a truculent landlady
Gives him a bill for the furniture which will have to be burned afterwards.
And the rage against the dying light that always falls on the carer – Keats's
Paranoia galloping alongside his consumption and 'the bitterness beyond
    aloes'
Turning to 'savageness' – food and drink flung away . . . and even his books
. . . His beloved books . . . *Shakespeare*. On the slow agonising road to
    nothingness
Nothing consoles. Bitter, bitter the lingering death. With the daisies on
    the ceiling
And the devils on the fireplace . . . and all the time, through the window
Onto the piazza ('I am sickened at the brute world . . . I hate men and
    women'),
The laughter of strangers pausing by the fountain's ceaseless song.

THE *PALAZZO*

The *palazzo* of masterpieces was covered in scaffolding but a great door, ajar,
Led to a dark atrium. Just a little light from an overgrown courtyard beyond.
Imposing stairs beckoned – but a peeved official came from an office to point.
Scrawled on a torn page the one word: *Chiuso*. It's supposed to be *open*,
I wanted to shout . . . but felt once again the futility of demanding fair play.
This *palazzo* was a mouldering dowager embittered by memories of jewels
Under chandeliers and the scented flesh gracefully moving to music . . . reduced
To caprice and pique, hoarding the treasure. Just like my aunt in her rank lair,
Smirking: 'I might leave it all to a dogs' home.' I left, raging inwardly, 'As if
I ever wanted your money – I pay my own way,' and never spoke to her again,
Thinking myself free and different but . . . I see it now . . . exactly the same . . .
Christ, get me out of this musty gloom . . . resentful, hard, miserly and unkind.

IV

AUTUMN BEGUILES THE FATALIST

LATE AFTERNOON ON THE PATIO

When sweetness surges up each stem
And every sheath-dress calyx proffers beauty to the sun
Oh then in the dark soil such fierce desires burn.
But too long a larva shame, buried and blind,
May make the blaze of wings too wild,
Too haphazard and crazed the late flight.

Now giddy with need and its own gorgeousness,
This butterfly hardly knows where next to flit.
It's all movement and colour . . . no substance,
No *core* . . . a sky petal with no parent flower,
Sail with no boat – windsurfer of air,
Flying flame without fuel, flirty fan with no girl,

Unaware even that one swat could bring it to earth
– The lumpen sour earth it so blithely disdains
In these flighty alightings, coy flutters and sways
As it postures all over the patio
Haunting the grey one who watches it silently
(What can a heavy heart tell a light head?)

Then the sun-spangled filigree web,
Finely tapering pampas grass blades,
Frothy lace gusset-pinned on the line
– So much taken for granted that ruptures
Reveal . . . as now, when a bird's sudden
Flight makes the shocked branch flail.

KNOTWEED

Eastern miniature daintiness also defunct,
Towering Japanese knotweed eclipses the sun
With rain-forest-dense burgeoning full of fierce sap,
Stems as thick as bamboo, leaves as broad as a hand
(And as richly veined), roots that break stone,
Big, undelicate blossoms that rear, pert and straight.

Rampant brute. Nothing kills it. It kills everything
(Flowers, bushes, grass, trees . . . other weeds).
It will strangle, asphyxiate and overrun
With a ruthlessness not just efficient
But zestful, exuberant . . . *Nietzschean.*
This thing's a weed *Übermensch*

Flaunting all we most hate about weeds,
Especially their terrifying absence of needs
(What needs nothing can take everything)
But also avid opportunism (appropriating
Fences, lines, drainpipes, walls, trees)
Their ability to take root and thrive *anywhere*

(Purple gypsy queen buddleia sprouting from eaves)
Their ferocious contempt for deterrent, constraint
(Endless brazen infringements, exultant returns)
And – the final affront – vivid beauty
That's never known feeding or care
Blithely putting to shame hothouse flowers.

Doubting, loath, we're not meant for such health
But to muddy, twist, deny and purge
By means of the oldest but still most effective
Consciousness–altering drug – words.
'Weedy', we say, to mean 'sickly and weak',
When there's nothing as healthy and strong as a weed.

Green conquistador, wild jungle weed,
You recall the mad strength I once had
– The delirium of requiring nothing,
Asking for nothing, receiving nothing,
Everything crucial supplied from within
By a pure exaltation, a dance of the soul.

OLD GOATS IN THE CÉVENNES

Forget gallops, lithe loping, long flowing manes.
This old goat, lurching over loose stones, has legs
Like an early sixties coffee table, spindly and splayed
(So the bloated belly looks even more out of scale),

An arhythmically clacking tin bell,
Stumpy blunt horns that curve the wrong way,
Grungy car mat for coat,
Wino's sharp musk and straggly stained beard.

As though, after creating the noble beasts and just before
He died, a discouraged God came on some leftover bits,
In a mordant fit jammed them together
And bequeathed this absurdity to a meaningless world.

Just as unsublime, I toil up the slope on tired legs,
Sweating, hungover. Crazy to walk in such heat
And with a bunch of cranks who can't get on
(Main culprits two stubborn old billy goats).

Scowling the lined faces under sunhats and far apart
Knapsacks with dog dazers, cameras, binoculars, guides,
Brie-on-*pain-complet* sandwiches, spring water, fruit,
Tablets, creams to protect and heal, tissues, wet wipes.

At the top a short rest to watch the village below,
Paper factory, mining and spinning long gone,
Many houses abandoned or grievously worn,
Bits of scrap metal shoring up rotten wood doors,

Concrete patches imperfectly mending old stone
(But wall lizards not short of dark homes),
The *boulangerie-épicerie* closing at one
Its chaotically half-filled shelves

(Though even before that the *patronne*
May turn from some customer old as herself
And with undisguised relish announce
That the rest of her bread's been reserved).

It seems this is one way to grow old
– To be shed by the unobliging world
And to warp into something inflexible and odd.
Fretful, sore, scarcely renewed, we resume

Though the path's petered out, the marked *randonnée's* lost.
Which the stubborn lead goat won't admit.
Surely squabbles in youth never festered like this?
Something densely recalcitrant grows with the years.

Sclerotic, cold, the buoyant heart becomes a stone.
Oh God, I pray, lift it, let honey gush forth.
Restore the path, carelessly lost, underfoot.
Offer weak eyes the symbols to show the way home.

Answer of course comes there none
– Or just this: amplified
And prolonged by the clear air and hills,
Cross old goats bleat and tin bells toll.

THAT CHICKEN

After the summer of surfeit, the wine-and-piano-accordion-accompanied
Noisy pavement-table meals, it is time to return to my spiritual exercises
– Sitting out on the patio with black coffee watching the railway-line
    weeds.

The strength and grace and gloss of weeds! And I see I've maligned
    the trees
By describing them as 'crooked'. They emerge sideways out of the
    embankment
But at once grow straight up. The leaves, gamely hanging on, stir in
    the breeze,

Fitful, light, though with a touch of September astringency providing
    that sense
Of imperilment I like. We always feel more intensely when threatened
    by loss.
Teaching soon . . . when The Sun will be what baseball hats read in class.

Ah here he comes again, the white-haired old man in the dark three-
    piece suit,
Cycling down the village street in the fierce heat of noon, very slow
    and stiff
But straight-backed and dignified, carrying a live chicken under his arm.

DISTURBANCES OF AUTUMN

Are the trains heavier . . . or the house jumpier?
At night floors tremble, panes rattle, bookcases quake.
Again now. To the window. *Too late.*

Above the track, crushed cans and thickets of weeds,
Pale imperfect growth framed by involuntary loss
– A gibbous moon among the half-bare trees.

BLACK COFFEE

Now even the tree on the corner, lithe swayer,
Whose sensitive tips swept the soul up to Heaven,
Has its limbs hacked to stumps by a brutal tree surgeon
And huddles forlornly in post-trauma shock.

When the grey has attained uncontested dominion
What exemplar can give us the faith to go on?
All the chroniclers of high deeds are mute on this one.
The struggle with sameness is not a good yarn.

Stay indoors and worship the one worthy maker
– The inscrutable cowled coffee-maker from Krups
Which, after long pondering and an equivocal cough,
Yields a wavering thread, black and bitter as truth.

HOPPER

Staring in through a window as a voyeur . . . or gazing out of one in
  yearning
– But on no occasion looking in the eyes of another. Can the light over
  city
And sea bring redemption? The disappointment varies from mild to severe.
He: *It could be I am not very human.* She: *Men are such ungrateful creatures.*
And they have disappointed not just themselves but *their homes.* In disgust
That they promised so much but delivered so little, these houses and rooms
Have gone dead and surrendered to air, light and shade. A sly wind disturbs
The white curtains. Ironic sun illuminates mundanity and tawdriness.
  (Partial
Redemption in noticing this?) Time is passing of course – simultaneously
With agonising slowness and frightening speed. The woman's naked body
Seems youthful . . . but has aged in indefinable ways. Waiting . . . waiting . . .
The drama not yet begun . . . or having an intermission . . . or suddenly
  over.

THE CONTAINER

Never mind the ruined factory over the dip.
Concentrate on this path, plunging, pitted,
Stone-strewn and encroached on by thorn bushes
Flaunting as blossoms torn white plastic bags.

Down it drops to the course of the stream
Where we came to hunt for sticklebacks
– A stream long blocked or buried
Under muddy waste ground.

The questing boys are still here though.
– Today standing round a container
Which squats on the bed of the banished stream.
Oppressive, armoured, tall and sheer,

It refuses to yield any secrets
However it's booted and battered with sticks
(All over it the names of frustrated knights:
Dinkleberry, Warhead, Macker, Skeets).

Now the leader gets a scotchie up and dances on top.
The rest cavort and howl with glee.
Even their furtive old mongrel yelps excitedly and leaps.
It would certainly seem to be a victory of sorts

But the few adult passers-by don't look across,
Continuing hunched against the drizzle
Which seems to be insidiously pacing itself
To endure to the end of the universe

Or at least till its message is deep in the bone:
You will spend your life at menial tasks for those you despise,
Endure continual disappointment, age and shrivel prematurely,
Die with everything undiscovered, unsaid and undone.

IN THE AGE OF THE DUVET

Many heavy coarse blankets, even heavier quilt – and often a coat on top
of that.
Like the weight of the world on young shoulders. No wonder we lay late
On grey afternoons as the sky like a dark candle-snuffer came down
And the Irish Greek chorus – rain – started its whisper: *Ye were born an*
eejit, look see, and an eejit ye'll die.
A blanket oppression removed suddenly. Instead, weightless airmail letters
buoyant with feathers.
And gone with the blankets those ponderous chests of drawers, wardrobes
and pattern-clogged walls.
Out with forbidding dark bulk in the new age of light!
No more burdens or bindings. Protection without restraint. Warmth
without weight.
In place of the sombre illusion of substance, the bracing illusion of airiness
– Cool space in whisper grey, lady blush, pale orchid, mountain mist.
    'Heavy' means 'threatening' now. Lightness is all.
So why am I still late beneath my light duvet with something immoveable
and dense in my soul?
Too soon for the Irish this weightlessness (Guinness Lite failed to take off).
We remember the clabber that clings to the boots. We remember the suck
of the avid earth.
This house where I lie is not flying but swiftly subsiding in treacherous clay.
When the loss adjuster sent me a builder from Galway I knew it was
Destiny, I knew it was Fate.
Though I thought a 'trial hole' would be a scientific thing, gleaming tubes
gliding in with hypodermic-like ease.
It took a pit big enough for him to stand in and shovel heavy, sour,
yellowish filth. *Where der's muck der's shit,* he said and grinned,

As though only too happy to renew his acquaintance with an old friend
the cities would love to expel.

Later I pressed him for explanations. Shovelling extra sugar into his tea, he
gave me a shrewd assessing peer.

Then he laughed and marked a line across his huge neck: *I only work from
here down.*

NOVEMBER

'White hair and solemn mug don't make a sage,' he warns,
Sinking on a sofa in the lounge with a sigh.
'Outer order and calm that inner tumult may rage.'
Long and inscrutable then his gaze on the patio
Where a dank greenish mould colonises the flags.

'What age brings is not wisdom,' he continues, 'but selfishness.
The five minutes left must be mine, mine . . . *all mine.*'
Further pause. Until, suddenly: 'People and wants. Endless wants.
No one's easy to live with . . . yourself least of all.'
The accused sky grey . . . worn . . . an old elephant's hide.

'Self-justification!' he cries. 'There's man's glory and pride,
Evolution's true crown, gift of even most dim.
What remarkable sophists we are to shift blame
And convince ourselves that whatever we crave we *deserve.*'
Fitful rain marks the window with short dotted lines.

Abrupt laugh. 'No more insects at least. No more bites
To go bad. An end to the real, if not the figurative, itch.'
Irony, winter sun, lights his bleak face.
'Life, denied, finds a way . . . makes us pay.
Though my eyes are long dry, my skin weeps.'

MY BRIEFCASE

Like its owner, it now sags a bit
– Two front pockets like bags under eyes,
Stitching gone, scored and stained, edges frayed,
Though the dark brown's old-furniture rich

And the inside's surprising – not musty and drab
But a light brown, bright, furry to touch,
With a living scent and secret pouch.
An intense inner life – and so no need to pose.

When it's empty it just flops and lolls.
Then accepts in its accommodating bosom
Huddled hungry masses yearning for A's
– A hundred illiterate exam scripts.

My old slimline executive case would have burst
. . . Or seriously creaked and groaned at least.
It had no give, could never hang loose,
The sharp corners jabbed knees, the twin lock

Catches sprang to attention like Swiss Palace Guards
And the combination locks I never bothered to use
In the end took to *locking themselves* to get
Noticed and win approbation (fat chance).

The relief at discovering a partner of
Adaptability, forbearance and commodiousness!
Like the greatest of books (*Moby-Dick*, *Ulysses*),
It accepts *everything* and will go *anywhere*

Even to teach Information Systems to accountants
In the building where Pound gave his lectures
On troubadour poets – *The Spirit of Romance* –
Even on visits to placement students

In the new-town technology parks with fish ponds
 – Or a Portakabin at the back of a Victorian hospital
Where a boss gave my youth a malevolent grin:
'Oh we'll soon knock the student out of him'.

Compadre, once more it is time. Another dirty cold dawn
To match the disabused heart. Needing help to get by,
In your redolent depths I place two clementines, a ham roll,
And contemporary poetry – a selection from Shakespeare

On nature and nurture, law and order, power and authority,
Bastard's rights, hating asylum-seekers, *amour fou*,
Loser rage, date rape, sleaze and the inevitability of ageism:
'Men shut their doors against a setting sun'. *Oof!*

Even so, adjusting the saddle-bag flap
And feeling hide on my thigh, I think . . . *horse*
(In relationships long-term and close
The apparent bearer's often the borne)

And hence western hero, the *hombre*
With probity, style, self-reliance, resolve.
Oh of course I'm too old for that stuff
 – But wasn't Randolph Scott *always* too old?

. . . And Cooper was *ancient* in *High Noon*.
In any case I saddle up, laconic and cool.
It's a desert with hostiles no *force* could survive
 – But a lone rider might just slip through.

AUTUMN BEGUILES THE FATALIST

Like a writer in a Hollywood film, blocked, enraged,
Nature rips the dead sheets from her Remington,
Viciously scrunches them and hurls them away.

When all values are relative, what can be said?
Is this how it must end, she accuses herself,
Our lush world a bleak space of unstable texts?

A catastrophic disempowerment! Irreversible decay!
How did such sovereign lusciousness wither and fade?
Who can tell where it went wrong? Can nothing be saved?

And now night falls so quickly on dark days of rain.
Trembling globules of mercury shimmer on panes.
Gravid hanging drops slowly engorge, quake and fall.

All the green bounty stripped, flooded, trampled to mush.
Disorder, foreboding, uncertainty, waste.
Grey mutating wraiths drift past the wind-shaken glass.

Bubbles dart round the tops of the pools on the street
As if to dodge the grim rods . . . but the rods snuff them out.
So much for evasion and ludic wit.

At last there dawns a bright dry day.
My darling and I venture out . . . warily.
Imbibe . . . and are intoxicated straight away.

This transparent fiery liquor was being distilled all the time!
Senses tingle alive. Torpid spirits revive.
Connections, leaps and correspondences are suddenly made

In a scalpel-sharp dry Scandinavian wind,
Cryosurgical fire which excises, elides,
Makes a tingle of possibility dance in the purified mind.

Again wonders and signs may be vouchsafed the loath.
A Messiah might come to the secular sane
And mysterious grace bless the disabused earth.

All along the stony bank between the railway line and path,
Still mauve-bloomed though sere of stem, Michaelmas daisies
    defiantly toss.
Lift the legs, head and eyes! Despair hates a brisk walk.

The life-enhancing keen clarity of mature scepticism
And my darling's invigorating late optimism
– Both have their perfect objective correlative

In this November Saturday, pellucid, serene,
Finally reconciled to what's been and what has to be
– With a beauty more subtle than that of the spring.

Autumn darling, your goodness is limpid and pure.
Now my old friends who loved my odd mind prefer you.
As I do! Cold sequestered hearts open to goodness not sweet.

Lambent mischief and gaiety dance in your eyes,
Providing at once the effervescence and essential dash of astringency
– Both the lemon slice and sparkle in the cool G&T .

V

THE DRUNKENNESS OF THINGS
BEING CARIOUS

THE DRUNKENNESS OF THINGS BEING CARIOUS

'Eat your five pieces of fruit,' my love says, 'keep corruption at bay.'
So with failing eyes I peer about, pick up a tangerine, reel from its
Circle of grey ash, thin ring of white rime and broad ring of brown mush
And feel the drunkenness of things being carious. World is rottener
Than we fancy it. The most cunning and implacable of colonists
Is decay. And all the outer wear, the corroding and crumbling and fraying,
Is merely diversion, street theatre. The real work's within, where disguised
Agents infiltrate, hoodwink defenders and wreck DNA. So even armour's
No help. The shiniest carapace cracks. Wings of course wither first.
But aren't books incorruptible armour, eyes, wings? What made
Me soar and see? What gave me strength? I take down from the shelf
One of youth's sacred texts . . . sere and spotted with age like myself.

SECOND CHILDHOOD

In the phrase 'second childhood' more meanings each year.
So it's *hi again* to old friends like raging demand, solipsistic
Impatience, desire to be looked after, bowel-centric happiness,
Forgetfulness, catnapping, fright at loud noises, the dark, biting
Anything hard (like a Shakespeare king, you fear for your crown)
And the comfort of incessant repetition (breakthrough moment
When you hear yourself retelling the *same* story to the *same* person
. . . *And realise you don't care*). Soon ever more daring escapes
From the tyranny of the real to the childhood paradise of dream
– At the checkout queue head deaf and blind to the cash-rich
But time-poor who rage just behind as you gaze down in
Mystical wonder at a purse full of dust and small change.

PSALM

Unworthy, Lord, mired in iniquity (I use the Disabled Toilet
Handbasin in work as a bidet), I come, craven, shamefaced,
To beg that you deliver me from aridity of spirit and restore
My old demonic zest. For my love has just confessed that
This was what made her wet. Therefore hear the voice of my
Supplications. Quicken me with deviance. Let mordant mockery
Dance in my eyes and a patina of irony lustre my words,
Let me seem to float on rebel angel wings above the world,
Pouring scorn on its shibboleths and idols of clay . . . but also
Unearthing obscure excellence. I was prince of espousals
Too once. Lord, the ferocity of those young enthusiasms
– Almost as good as contempt for alarming the dull.

THE SECOND CHANCE

'This kid has balls . . . I like that,' chuckled the gang bosses
In the movies – convincing us that the world would be charmed
By a youthful audacity and impertinence (a subset of the larger
Illusion that one's shortcomings, wholly unlike those of others,
Are amusingly cute). As if the world would be amused:
'Who does this upstart think he is? Bury the fucker. Lose him.
Let him go white-haired in the wilderness brooding on
The opportunities he enjoyed and the second chance he won't.'
The second chance! *Aware*, this time. But maybe we'd fare
Even worse. Maybe I'd be tempted to network, seek out
Powerful mentors, kiss ass. Knowing what I know now,
Where would I find the nerve for that sublime insolence?

WHY SATAN LOVES THE OLD MOVIES

So enthralling those scenes where nobility casts out the venal
And cleaves to integrity. Virile, majestic Burt Lancaster:
We were the lions. After us come the jackals. My answer is *no*.
But 'Yes yes,' cries the audience, 'bring us hard costly decisions.
We'll take them unflinchingly, straight-backed and bold-eyed'.
And 'Yes yes,' cries Satan, who loves these old movies, 'believe
In and raptly await The Great Choice. While it fails to arrive,
Time can do its dark work. As if I'd waste valuable resources
On *theatre*. Time is my secret enforcer. Those heroes, so upright
And bold in plush seats, they'll come and *beg* to sell their souls
When backs start to be stooped and eyes dulled by the endless
Petty degradations of the strength-and-spirit-sapping years.'

THE MENTOR ODE

Oh of course they're old bores, these ubiquitous, grave provincial poets
    of ours,
But you don't have to go around insulting them, Iccius. These fits of
    spleen damage
Only yourself. Instead, take as a mentor one shrewd and well placed, who
    knows
How things are done . . . and set to work to flatter him. No, *wait*. It's not
    crass.
Remember that flattery too is an art. Far from easy, as everyone seems
    to assume,
It can even *repel* if too blatant and crude. It takes insight to pinpoint
    precisely
The praise people ache to hear, literary talent to phrase it effectively, timing
To know when to use it and humour to smooth away lingering
    awkwardness.
In fact just like poetry, Iccius. Art that looks artless, spontaneous, genuine.
And to *use* one of these wily old birds is fun. You can ditch him when
    your
Own career starts to bloom, which it will, in just the *natural* way you desire
(And it always deserved), with the inevitability, plenitude and rootedness
    of a tree.

UNHAPPY AS LARRY

Larry McCoubrey — even the name resonated with reassuring down-to-
  earth bonhomie
And his public persona was jocund and blithe — but the face I met for the
  radio interview
Was a cold mask of broken veins and rancorous eyes. Of the legendary
  silver tongue
Not a trace. Taciturn. Until, suddenly: 'I'm a sports commentator as well . . .
  and every
Saturday afternoon I'm sitting up there' — he indicated angrily a booth in
  the sky —
'Up there in front of *twenty thousand* or more.' The implication seemed to
  be that by
Interviewing me he was *risking his life*, that some enraged sniper would
  make him pay.
For *my* jokey magazine piece? Vain youth that always believes itself
  prime cause.
I understood not even youth, much less middle age, disappointment,
  performing or fear.
So Larry, sour, slumped at the mike — but the instant the green sign came
  on *he* came on,
Like a Christmas tree, all tinsel brilliance and coloured lights: 'Now,
  Michael Foley . . .'
So abruptly and so monstrously jovial that I flinched as though he'd pulled
  out a knife.

THE HATEFUL THING

There was time, always time . . . time for the world to repent and oblige.
But I understand now that, not just is the world unaware of a sin,
Its current gifts, so meagre seeming, might be withdrawn.
And so I feel the bite of the hateful thing. Lord, that it should
Come to this. Lowest, basest of base. I have to whisper it – *envy*.
The old bitter bleats: *Why him and not me? I'm as good as him at least.*
That I, who was my own sun and blazed in solipsistic ecstasy
(If I energised anything else it was by accident), should crave
The meretricious sun of krieg lights. Smite me, Lord. Strike me down.
Rub my face in the dust to remind me of vanity and nothingness.
We are dust, however painted, prinked, spotlit and hotly applauded
. . . Dust, *dust*. Though it frolics in sunbeams, the dust remains dust.

WE ARE AT MUCH UNEASE

Our grim secret – the deep self's a quivering, terrified, raw,
Stunted thing. *Security, security, security*, it shrieks
But there are only the degrees of insecurity, disguises more
Or less effective, people more or less blind. Fierce dissembling
Is needed full time (who wants in touch with an inner dwarf?)
So choose your style – brazen assurance (pre-emptive strike),
The people's defence team of banality and facetiousness
Or for those who avoid the mob – ironic detachment
(The classiest front and hence mine). All of these are hard work.
And hence also craving for comfort, indulgence, sedation, respite
– The sofa snug as a mother's lap, indirect light to massage
The unquiet spirit and, sweeter than Mozart, the tinkle of ice.

GOD'S DEPRESSION

God isn't dead, merely old and ignored. Who now knows or cares that
    He suffers
From indecision, panic attacks, short-term memory loss, chronic fatigue
    (narcolepsy
On chairs but insomnia in bed), despairing thoughts of insubstantiality and
    worthlessness
(He looks up the proofs of His own existence in secret), anhedonia,
    boredom, aporia
And failure of zeal and nerve (He's attended anger-management classes
    for wrath)?
So He's often withdrawn and morose, very 'down', loath even to rise on
    these days
That grow steadily dimmer and greyer while ever more bright blaze the
    days of creation,
Of fire, vision, grace . . . master plan and detail. All is boredom without
    exaltation.
Might He settle for praise? He hears only demand and complaint. So
    refreshing
That labour, so wearing this leisure. So teeming the void and so vacant
    the world.
When did everything change? How could *certainty* fade? Where's the faith
    to go on?
So burdensome the emptiness of relativism . . . and so weightless the
    tablets of stone.

GOIN' OFF FISHIN'

Their lazy presumption – that any boy would love to go fishing
With his father. But I hated the pervasive wet, rain mist on glasses,
Mud that clung in heavy clumps to the boots, dripping bushes
And brambles, black nymphless trees, cow dung and slippery stiles
To be lurched over weighed down by waterproof clothing and boxes, tins,
Bags, rods and nets. Always *I* carried nets. *They cast nets on my soul.*
But not on fish. I never caught anything . . . or saw anything caught
– Or even hooked. So worse again the empty-handed taciturn trudge back
Through the fading light and insidious drizzle, with the grim premonition
That this might be life, a series of compulsory profitless rituals
In which you were alone with your inchoate dream, possibly never
To take final form . . . much less be acknowledged and acted upon.

THERE'S NO CALL FOR THE HALF OF IT

'*Jesus Mary and Joseph!*' my mother would screech, when I asked her for
  ten bob
For a dance or an LP, 'you'll have us in *Stubbs*.' As always I learned what
  this meant
Only much later – *Stubbs's Gazette* of bankrupts and debtors. Never
  thought to ask
At the time of course. No one explained anything, least of all teachers.
  Though now
I can see why not. What more could anyone need to know? Everything
  was either
Compulsory or forbidden. 'There's no call for the half of it,' she snapped
  if you
Wanted something. 'You've a lot to be thankful for', if you asked awkward
  questions.
But *her* question – 'And where will that get ye?' – was wise. For I left to
  pursue
Explanations . . . but found only irony – e.g. this mother was post-modern
  poetry's
Unsung precursor in hatred of answers and love of evasion, suggestion,
  foreboding,
Non sequiturs, gnomic banal. My lost birthright . . . *priceless* . . . her solemn
  look,
Turning from questions to black Irish cloud mass: 'That's like *a big plump*.'

THE GREAT BOOKS

In the velvet-curtained parlour aunts studied great books. But not classics
of literature
– Wallpaper books . . . massive ledgers of samples, thick, stiff pages, dark-
patterned,
Deeply embossed. Both caressed like Braille and scanned like the Cabbala.
Lingering
Fingers turned pages reluctantly, with sweet indecisive sighs at richness of
choice
('Sacred Heart, Ah'm in *swithers*') and cries at correspondences thrilling as
Baudelaire's
('That would go well with the rug in the front room'), while, disdainful as
Baudelaire,
I sneered in a corner. I would seek all these pudding women strove to
suppress,
Walk the bitter night, plumb the abyss, delight in squalor, infamy,
drunkenness,
Discover and publish unwelcome harsh truth. Two extreme vanities in one
little room,
Already overstuffed with furniture. Dense, rich, *bizarre*. Now they're
gossiping,
Books laid aside. Faces bright. I can't hear. Back . . . *oh back* . . . just to
listen and look.
What does it matter which way we turn? Faced or denied, it's all lost just
as soon.

IMMINENCE

In that first city summer of shimmering heat *every* Underground station
was Adlestrop,
Eerily pent . . . and *on every trip*. But especially Finchley Road where, no
whit less fair
Than a rose garden, buddleia burgeoned on waste ground and across the
track I saw
A girl waiting, so sensitive, yearning and disconsolate that I wanted to cry
out:
'I'm the one you seek, merely disguised as a gauche Irish barman. Your
kiss will
Bring forth a prince, gracious and eloquent. Plus, I can open two bottles
at once
With one hand. Be the eighth light tonight in *The Seven Stars*.' Never.
There were
No adventures. Nothing happened. It didn't matter. The true joy was
imminence.
In the corridors of the Underground currents of balmy air, zephyrs from
paradise,
Fondled my hair and on the escalator up to the lurid night a warm breeze
caressed
The face I turned towards advertisements for lingerie and new plays,
guarantors of
An end to the age of concealment, when the flesh and the spirit would
both be revealed.

KICK OFF THE SLIPPERS

In Van Hoogstraten's *Pantoufles* an open latch door shows a dishcloth and broom,
Then another door onto a hall where a pair of dropped slippers mar shining floor tiles.
A third door, also open (dangling bunch of keys dark as a scrotum), admits to a room
Whose gold-cloth-covered table bears candle and book and, above these, a view of
An enigmatic young woman facing a bed. Indecisive? Bored? Ruminant? Waiting?
No, *wait*. Is she *even in there at all*? Mirror . . . or *painting*? Just around the corner
. . . Or entirely imagined? And why are you even considering this? You ought to be
Sweeping up, drying the dishes. Trespass would bring only trouble – or emptiness.
Though what if you're not an invisible drudge but *the chosen* whose moment has
Finally come (and will not come again)? What if this is *the test*? The locked door
Left wide open . . . the radiant threshold . . . the path to the altar with candle and book
. . . And above all the resonant palpable silence . . . The inanimate seems to urge
The petrified heart – drop the broom, kick the slippers off, cross over, *pass beyond*.

105

THE CITY

'At least here you're among your own kind,' someone says with a satisfied grin

...And immediately you want to board the nearest train ... to *anywhere* ...

But probably the city, sanatorium of oddities with a phobia for belonging, analeptic

Its graffitied streets and piss-perfumed alleyways. Where it's easy to lose yourself

Trying to find yourself. And as for what it costs to call a plumber out at weekends

When Denise's friend Danny would have fixed it for nothing. Then the free spirits,

Boozing and joking and screwing, reveal themselves. *Listen, there's money in* ...

From venality masked by facetiousness you turn to the window's patch of blue

By the top of some old building with hello-sailor cherubs holding out Grecian urns

And ferocious lion heads clenching wreaths in their teeth. Why *these* and why *there*

Where no one sees from the street – or the building itself? Ah the joys of perversity.

Solitary, mute in the clamour and multitude, only belonging where no one belongs.

SPUD IN THE GOB

It was one of those mansion blocks, darkly austere, I've always wanted to
    live in myself
But they're meant for more interesting types – ex-dictators, spies, arms
    dealers, politicians'
Mistresses, madames of incredibly specialised brothels and bad-tempered
    European émigrés
With ear hair and boxed sets of Wagner. Then these people – was I
    imposing? No one
Answered the entry phone. Try other bells? The response you'd expect –
    distant, crackly,
Impatient and curt. Abruptly I was stricken by spud-in-the-gob, that
    affliction attacking
The Irish in England. It feels as though, just as you open your mouth to
    speak, someone
Has crammed a large, dirt-caked, misshapen potato right into it, so all you
    can utter's
A guttural croak. I peered in at the lobby. Two sombre plants flanked the
    cool marble tiles.
Art Deco wall lamps discreetly cupped light. Dim and silent. No,
    something was coming.
The lift, disconcertingly modern . . . which opened on empty gun-metal-
    grey steel.
For a moment it sat like that . . . gleaming. Then the doors shuddered shut
    and it rose.

LORD, HOW ARE THEY INCREASED THAT TROUBLE ME

So already I'm running late and, as soon as I step out, ahead is
The little fat baldie from the luxury block – a car man who must have
Been ordered to walk i.e waddle. *Agony!* Hang back – or catch him
And have to make small talk . . . in this bleak November dawn . . .
To a Churchill-cigar-waving *nouveau* with two drooling Dobermans,
An unhappy son packed off to boarding school and a gross wife who
Farts during yoga in the Community Hall. And ahead the station's
Insolent beggar. 'Thanks a lot, sir,' he sniggers aggressively
When you pass by with a face like the death mask of Caesar.
Then the ticket-machine ditherers and the escalator blockers.
Where's the so-called frantic city pace? Lord, I acknowledge
The Glory of Creation – manifold even the occasions of morning rage.

THE VILEST MEN ARE EXALTED

How bleak a world, disabused veterans, if women refused
To placate angry men. Like this guy on the train with mad,
Sticking-up hair, glaring eyes, who swears, roots in his briefcase,
Stamps, flings down the case. To wake up next to *this*.
Yet *she* obviously did and is not repelled, soothing with that
Hey-it-isn't-so-bad-and-besides-I-adore-you-still look.
No beauty . . . *better* – intelligent, frisky, illuminated . . . an *angel*.
Who actually moves her face in for a kiss . . . and the bastard
Averts his head, rolls it impatiently, as if to relax a stiff neck.
What he needs is a kick in the scrotum. Halt this train at once!
I must rush home and hold my beloved, weep, beg her
Forgiveness. 'I need to atone.' 'For what?' 'Being a *cunt*.'

DON'T JUST DO SOMETHING, SIT THERE

Fulsome late light ennobles the railway-line trees and lays
A warm saffron burnish on pallid bindweed. Now even
The neurotic thrush sits, reconciled, in the fraught leaves
Which fluttered all day but have yielded at last to
A still sky effulgent with gold, as the sun, mighty autarch,
Dissolves and flows. The answer is quietism, everything says.
Just descend to a deep place below spume and froth.
Purge desire and regret. Concentrate on the breath.
From the abdomen breathe slowly . . . in, out . . . out, in . . .
Relax limbs, empty mind . . . the impossible part.
Find the blackest thing, gurus say, and focus on that
. . . But what's blacker (and less quietist) than my heart?

THIS WORLD OF THRALL

On the patio at evening with a G&T, watching the charcoal burn nicely
  down,
God in His Heaven and the meat in the marinade . . . for company, fair
  queen
And trusty retainers – my inner dwarf, hyena, clown and, latest friend, corpse.
Ah how blessèd are we that are not simple men! Mild velleities of twilight
And the tinkle of ice. Hour of secret things, murmurs and sighs. I'm wrong.
God's in the world . . . in these clouds and weeds . . . and (suddenly I
  understand
Their strange power) the grinning soft animals on the secretaries' work
  stations.
I am finally in touch with my inner high priest. In the legendary lost land of
Ataraxia I was a priest. Then my lips knew the nectar of vacuity and my ears
The haunting song of the abyss. But the idols of activity and entertainment
  killed
The old faith. After food we'll go in for the TV glass. Saints, mystics,
  murderers,
Everyone now wants a 40-inch flat screen. No longer can anyone vanquish
  the world.

DAY OF REST

On the seventh day you linger in bed and refrain from unnecessary labour
By requesting a nice little toss-off instead. The voluptuousness of that final
Warm doze! Late the rising for bacon and eggs – but organic, free range,
Bacon grilled and eggs poached – because you intend to live forever
In variety and ease . . . and hence scour the sections on Life Style,
Health, Holidays, Property, Cash. Later on, watch *A Place in the Sun*.
Would you go for the renovated old-town apartment or the fabulous
Views from the mountain home? Sheez, already it's aperitif time!
Chunky cold tumbler, music of ice. Coonawarra Shiraz with the meal.
And a port with the evening TV, where a short-tempered, maverick
Police officer with a foundering relationship and an alcohol problem
Solves, with daring, unorthodox brilliance, the crime.

EPISTLE

Brethren, verily I say unto you (from the patio of my second home in
    the sun)
That should you discover all knowledge and wisdom, without cash reserves
You are null . . . and that even unlimited disposable income will bring no
Contentment unless you are known. For if you should speak with the
    tongues
Of angels but testify in sordid obscurity it will captivate less than a toilet
    flush.
Moreover, brethren, I would not have you ignorant of the power of the flesh.
Are we not carnal men? And what doth it profit a man to have wealth
    and renown
If the tabernacle of the temple of the Holy Ghost, his G-spot, is never
    found?
Therefore cultivate above all attractiveness and should the flower of your
    age seem
To wilt you must reinforce its natural defences with Daily Renewal
    Cleansing Milk.
For sex illuminateth, sex surpasseth all things. Now abideth sex, money
    and fame,
These three – but in this Holy Trinity sex of course reigns supreme.

THE AGE OF ENTITLEMENT

I thought I was remarkably fortunate in having as supervisor, God,
But when we met to discuss the thesis someone knocked at His office door.
'Well *of course* that's an obstacle,' I heard Him say. 'But also a *challenge*.
Whatever stands in the way must become The Way.' The seeker stormed off
But God, unbothered, jocular, cried down the corridor, 'Suspect any
Solution that requires you to do nothing.' Then back to me. 'Your topic?'
Nervously I muttered it: 'The Age of Entitlement'. He nodded, pondering.
'But after the colon, what?' 'Obligation's journey from within to without.'
'Stinging! Valid! Already I'm seeing a *major book*.' Second knock. This time
He was testier. 'Yes I am *well aware* that I'm God but, *no,* making *you* happy
Is *not* my job.' More resentful muttering. Divine impatience: 'Listen, Jack,
Who do you think you are – *Buddha*? Settle for comfort, possessions and food.'

THE ZORBA OF THE NORTH

They that have wasted us require of us mirth and song.
Hence the restaurant location map with my boss's email.
'A Greek place with a band – come and do Zorba's Dance!'
And try to charm the new colleague – slim, dark, husky-voiced?
With a life-affirming Zorba laugh. But too loud and too long.
And she stands too close. Something false . . . or is it me?
Again too cold and loath? Often now a shade comes forth
And sadly scratches curly locks: 'There's a meanness of spirit
About you, Mickey.' Always this diminutive to soften reproach
In our heated but friendly disputes (I cared enough to argue then).
Jimmy, I still can't believe you're dead, lover and singer,
Sole Sun King of rain-sodden Ulster, only Zorba of the North.

THE TROUBLE

The age bonus – honour and dignity? *Peufff!* Grotesquerie
Will harry us into the earth. At my mother's last hospital bed
May McCafferty, homely face framed in a frizzy perm:
'Winnie, it's the Padre Pio relic ye wanted' – too insensitive
To note Winnie's mortification. That her rational son should have
Witnessed this . . . *voodoo.* Quick snatch . . . and under the pillow.
May, lingering: 'Remember now, Mrs Barr wants it tomorrow
– And by the way, what is she in for?' 'Oh *tests* . . . I'm not sure.'
For six decades Winnie's frown banished the gross, enforced
Taste and decorum. Now into her final bed climbed smirking
Demons as, beaming insanely, May leaned close to murmur:
'Winnie, *I* think the trouble's at the partin' ay 'er legs.'

THE HEGEMONY OF NOW

So you go back to that corner place . . . and find *the entire corner* gone.
Instead a bar, a vast and brazen *arriviste*, assured as its patrons
At pavement tables for whom it's *you* who shouldn't exist – pathetic,
Feeble, old shade. Well, who would summon ghosts or any immaterial thing
Where sunshine pours through picture windows into airy spaciousness
With natural blond wood furniture and floors, paintings of bold shapes
In primary colours, poles offering intelligent and outspoken journals,
Great machines producing coffee and attractive professionals sipping wine?
The hegemony of now asserts its power through ease, transparency and light.
Where in such brightness could maleficence lurk? Suddenly a flare-up
Of flame and smoke! No, it's not the lords of destruction declaring
Themselves – just a chef in the open-plan kitchen area flambéing steak.

SQUEEZED

It was one of those bright summer evenings in the city, with more fire
And splendour than actual heat (and the finer for that) and we were strolling
Down a side street to a rendezvous with old friends for an aperitif and meal
When, abruptly, a hand stopped me dead, took savage hold of me and
   squeezed
Ferociously, terminally . . . as a lemon is squeezed . . . forcing out burning
   tears.
A heart attack, it seemed . . . and in a way it was. For when it eased I saw
That this was the route from my day to my evening job twenty-five years
   before
And I mustn't have passed here since that painful time. So back now it all
   came
. . . And back the woman herself, concerned, peeved. How explain? For this
Was that old horror, not to be mentioned ('No recriminations . . . ever'), but
   mixed
With strange pleasure . . . that a mind so controlled could be so hugely
   possessed,
That something . . . *anything* . . . could wring so much juice from old bones.

THE YEARS AND THE WORLD

Sore-eyed and fed up, I need a wild lover to perch on my lap,
Whip my glasses off, groan at the cruelly marked bridge
Of my nose and insist that I leave these old books. But alas,
My beloved's dispirited too . . . baffled, beaten down, lost . . .
I.e. just like the rest. And when even a hot-blooded gypsy queen
Loses her nerve who can face down the years and the world?
That most sickening feeling, betrayal, is what broke her heart.
How could *old friends* desert? This the chronicles prophesy
– That the worst will kiss power's ass, the best at best hide.
Confront or defy and you're on your own. And the clear-sighted
Chroniclers end with this: 'Don't expect Robin Hood's band
At your back. Every honest road leads to a cold lonely place.'

5 A.M.

As the hungry rat scuffles in the railway-line undergrowth
And an urban fox behowls the moon, the sleeping couple thrash
And groan. In his dream he is back in the first job of youth
And abasing himself once more before the hated bully boss.
While in *her* dream she can't find the meeting room . . .
And then the agenda folder's lost. Panicking, she snaps awake
– Knowing from experience she won't get back. The advice
Is not to try but to rise and make a soothing drink . . . which
Usually does the trick. Not tonight. Work looms. He snores.
The fox cries. Now the house shakes. It's some heavy, grinding,
Slow train. With what function or freight – so apparently reluctant
Yet inexorable, agonised and agonising the metal-on-metal shriek?

GOD'S INSOMNIA

What makes this 5 a.m. world so strange, she understands in sudden dread,
Is its fear of the insomnia of God. The world knows He's still up. Probably
Had one of His drinking nights, dropped into heavy unsatisfying sleep
And then woke for good at four – parched, aching, guilty, sour.
Now afraid of His wrath, the world, pale and fraught, holds its breath,
Hardly dares stir. And, fearful too, she creeps to the living room,
Forbearing to lift to lips her camomile tea. But mad Renee next door
Has a game show *full on*. Provoking a sleep-deprived, hungover God!
As the audience cackle like minions of Hell the wan street cringes
Into itself, not a leaf on the corner tree moves. But finally it ceases.
Even Renee's afraid. Retribution now surely. Everything tenses.
Agonisingly loud – the high echoing *ping* of a plug being pulled.

THE UNCLEAN MIASMAS OF RANCOUR AND BILE

To rise like a condor clearing the Andes with a mighty wingbeat,
Whose thunder makes the valley dogs howl and snap leads
And the terrified guanacos fling themselves from high peaks,
And to soar above offices, malls, monstrous stores by ring roads
(Each with cars in car parks packed efficiently as melon seeds)
High up into solitude and purity. For once again the visage of God
Is obscured by the unclean miasmas of rancour and bile
And the babble of wants and rants, grievances, fantasies,
Denials and lies. And I too a self-obsessed whinger. Deep space
. . . The void. *Home*. Remote, unsullied, silent at last (I'll make
A great neighbour, Lord), looking down from safe height
On the iniquitous earth – a cold eternal voyeur like the moon.

I STRUGGLE, LORD

I struggle, Lord, struggle . . . even to like my few friends.
And, as a losing army falls back into a stronghold, I abandon
Them to concentrate on my beloved, my queen. Yet with her too,
Sometimes. Well, you know the secret unconscionable iniquity
Of the heart . . . the thoughts even I wouldn't dare to write down.
I have to imagine life without her, friends already all gone,
Now finally and terminally alone, beating boards and howling,
Lord, that I would gladly give it all – the pension, house
And manuscripts – to enjoy just one more of those Saturdays
When we walked along the river all the bracing afternoon,
Then came upon an old inn where tired limbs were eased,
Glasses touched . . . and warm eyes met above the cold wine.

STEWART

And now Stewart's biography. It's him – but drained of colour and oddity.
The title should have been 'Stickin' Out', his constant phrase of approbation.
For Stoo Baby everything was stickin' out – even in murderous Belfast.
For me it was shite. So a hard-and-soft-cop team. Flaubert my man,
Mordant, pitiless, bleak. Stoo all for Scottie, in particular Gatsby.
When I criticised its implausible Victorian plot (even Chekhov hated
Ending with a shot), not to mention the central absurdity of a mob
Front man given unlimited wealth, Stoo just laughed. What could gainsay
Those aching last pages? Of course he was right. *Borne back ceaselessly* . . .
The Club Bar . . . on Monday nights . . . sweet disputation . . . *Scottie, Scottie!*
Flaubert! But agreement on one thing – the local scribes all safe careerists
. . . *Contemptible.* Instant duet of derisive shrieks. Stickin' out.

A PASSAGE TO ITHACA

'Come with me to the States,' he said, 'I'll get you work teaching writing.'
In Ithaca. *Ithaca!* I didn't even know what that meant. (Later I found out
– But no one was offering Ithaca then.) Safe after all, I turned him down
And came to London instead. Supposed to get settled, then ask him over.
Failed to write – careless. Cut to the last meeting. Everything had changed.
No more living on boiled eggs. Now he was in town with his hit play.
Meet at the theatre. Just the two of us, I assumed, but the cast were all there.
The male lead mimed reading reviews – cringing away in dread, then turning
Back to peer through a lattice of fingers. While the beautiful lead actress
    gushed:
'Stewart's a *genius.*' Well, they would go to work soon and the sceptical
Ulstermen would hoot at all this. But Stoo rose with them. 'I'm going in
To see the show.' His final words, not soft: 'You could have kept in touch.'

CHAMPAGNE

So I never knew how he negotiated the difficult later years of marital
Breakdown and the cancer's return. When I think of the dullards I've wasted
Time drinking with since, I could weep for my stupidity and carelessness.
Was it still stickin' out? Whatever armour we don, the corrosive years
Breach it and burn. Is the secret of youth insulation? You see things
. . . And understand some of them . . . but nothing can really *impinge*.
So there were constant explosions and riots, torturers in back rooms
And murderers cruising streets – but we'd stroll out in the evening
Like princes in the Tuileries. And one Monday night he came early
. . . Excited. The all clear! The seven years up today! Cancer defeated!
A bottle waved . . . some cheap sweet sparkling drink. Vile stuff
– But what did I know then? For me – for us both – it was champagne.

WINTER LIGHT

Winter and the white hairs in the mirror, Odysseus, make a loath heart
Yearn for hearth and home. But those loyal old servants and dogs are
  no more,
Your Penelope married the first suitor, started a new family and drove out
Telemachus, who's drifted off in alcoholic embitterment. As for the rest of
  them,
A gold cloak and a retinue might impress . . . but hardly one toiling man
  in soiled robes.
Who at home remembers a setting off? On the wine-dark sea you
  become a wraith.
They would look directly through you as though you didn't exist – and
  then even
Resourceful Odysseus would find it hard to go on. The only Ithaca is
  your nerve
And this you can find only here, in the strange city where you will never
  belong.
So fare forth once again, a little stiff the old legs but tumultuously full
The old head (more alive than most of these pumpkin heads) in winter
  light,
Late and brief, without durance or warmth, striking fire from high panes.

MINIONS OF THE MOON

Eerie cries waken me at 5 a.m. in dread. I pad to the window
And scan the street . . . scoured clean by moonlight . . . deserted . . .
Then from behind a car slinks, not the sleek cunning creature
Of fable, but a droop-headed, draggle-tailed, mangy old fox
Which crosses the street back and forth. Seeking what? Food?
A mate? The way home? That's long lost. Though it can't be
Fun to be an ageing scavenger under the bilious urban moon,
The rare morsels all snatched by the young. Baffled, hurt, but
Defiant the cry. It won't be anyone's pet. Autonomy and liberty
To the bitter end. Yes! However starved and disappointed,
Hoard wildness, *exercise it* . . . roam the lounge at night and cry:
'I am neither as others desire . . . nor what they think me to be.'

OLD FANTASTICAL DUKE OF DARK CORNERS

So be it, you have to cry out at last. The dukedom's usurped – and you
Won't get it back. (No one else even *knows* it's usurped, for Chrissake.)
No spirit will intervene. The only salvational tempest's within. So let
Inner tumult reign. It's the late crazy don't-give-a-shit time. You're *free*,
Unelect, untrammelled, free of the world and therefore free in the world
. . . . Toy of exiled dukes. Go forth. You don't even need the dark hood.
Age is nature's disguise. You're unrecognised and anonymous – old
Fantastical duke of dark corners, free to ferret, pry, eavesdrop, hypothesise,
Throw off weird koans like dirty shirts (no, *faster* – servantless dukes
Make a shirt last *three days*) and give counsel to sorely beset and vexed,
Especially women. O come to me, my moist angels. I'll listen, advise,
Grave and wise (though secretly stiff in my scandalous soiled pants).

SHOWTIME WITH GOD

'Seek . . . no, *demand* . . . and you will find,' insists God, removing the
  cellophane
From a pack of cards. 'It's the age of blind photographers and wheelchair-
  bound
Mountaineers. I mean, look at *me*. Shouldn't even *be here*. But I'm hard to
  dump.'
Glitter of mischievous glee. 'I persist . . . like the afterglow of a beautiful
  fuck.'
Chuckles, cuts and interleaves with bewildering speed. 'Though am *I*
  really *me*?
Jerk my long Santa beard. Hey, beatitude of the day: A white beard is a
  bitch
For eating vegetable soup. Who in these times to trust? Maybe even God
  cheats?'
Shaking, pulls and lets go an elasticated false beard. 'This much is true
  at least.
If you aren't in you can't win. So just watch my hands now.' Nimbly
  skims out
The pack, scoops it back. 'Though the closer you look, the stranger
  everything seems.
Is there a deeper mystery than the obvious?' Pauses for answers. Receives
  none.
'OK. Showtime with God.' Flicks a quick stylish fan. 'Pick a card . . .
  any one . . .'

THE MUSIC OF TIME

Time, said Hawking, runs backwards and is personal. But who didn't
    know that?
Tomorrow's a grey null, while forty-five years ago is increasingly bright . . .
    and my
Just-for-you clock makes a seminar last an eternity while semesters go by
    in a flash.
The only question is *how to fight back*. Play, as Earl Hines plays 'Indian
    Summer',
A gleeful revenger disrupting time (whose personal touch was to bury
    him . . . *twice*)
Exclusively on solo piano now (there's no wish, at sixty-nine, to
    collaborate further)
   . . . Though that's not the main point. It's to get at the thing *with your
    bare hands*,
Caress, jab and slam, tease and hammer chords to answer the grotesquerie
    of God
By means of irony, dissonance, percussive zest, missing-a-stair-in-the-dark
    pauses,
Populous runs, upper-register single notes carefully inset like precious
    stones
With, underneath all that, the rolling bass of squandered years, shame and
    regret:
Could have . . . *should have* . . . if . . . if . . . if . . . if . . . back . . . back . . .
    back . . . back . . .

LATE SENSUAL FRENZY

One bounty of age's impatience is abandonment of virtuosity,
Scrollwork and finish . . . e.g. the late sensual frenzy of Degas,
Picasso and Monet – time only for shape-fusing welters of colour
That nurture obsession (genitals, *nymphéas* and bathing women),
Banish perfection (slash, daub, drip and swirl, bits of canvas
Left bare) and never give *even a thought* to reception (do it for
Yourself and it's universal). Unserene, unsaintly, unreconciled,
These three howled like dogs for the look, taste and touch of
The succulent world. So stand a long time in front of their works
And feast your own dimming eyes, exhilarated and terrified,
On colours that rise off the canvas to float, shimmer, dance . . .
Gorgeous hallucination of the drowning before the dominion of black.

WINTER IN PARIS

First time in Paris in winter. Harsh lesson – old bones and sclerotic hearts
  need warmth
But our drab room was chilly – *adieu les ébats amoureux* – while a bitter
  wind scoured
Streets already all seen. No, a new gallery, new show – *Picasso Intime* –
  unconcessive,
Mad, late howls of love, lust and will. Death if need be but meantime no
  dying. So perhaps
We're still young? And the right work a poster for once – the Crazy Cock
  self-portrait,
Wild-eyed, in striped top. Disaster! My plastic *ne marche pas*. No art
  treasures . . . *robbed.*
Pockets, purse – just enough cash for catalogue, poster and even *deux*
  grands cafés noirs
In the space like a great *salle de bal* where my yes-to-life sweep
  accidentally felled
A fake potted plant, sending a green sphere of plastic leaves dancing across
  the dance floor
To the feet of the dark-suited *maître d'* . . . who laughed. Then once more
  winter's blast,
But in genitals, heart, head and elegant bag there was fire, fire, fire, fire –
  so we
Linked arms and boldly faced into it, down *Rue de Paradis* and *Passage du*
  Désir.

DAPPLED THINGS

Youth never knows what it gives or receives – and stiff age rarely kneels
– But Lord, Lord, I've cherished your bounty for once. This absurd husk
Can scarcely believe that the tropical paradise of the flesh has forgotten
To cast him from its breast. *There's someone still willing to let me.* I quake
. . . Like a tomb-robber avid for gold but in dread of some terrible curse.
Quickly then! Before someone remembers. Before night. Before winter
Sets in. Above all, before our teenage daughter gets home. Fleet as hers,
Our glad steps on the stair carpet threadbare from dolorous adult tread.
Quickly – but gratefully, tenderly, kindness for foreplay, accepting
The scars and wens and warts and the shyly blossoming liver spots.
Glory be to God for dappled things – but even so, draw down those
Blinds. Pull the comforting duvet across us in the orthopaedic bed.

WHEN WHAT WE HOPED FOR CAME TO NOTHING, WE REVIVED

Each time the bleakness seems terminal – faith and hope gone
From the graceless grey days. Unanointed, you go forth to win
Bread long stale, the heart cold and occluded but pierced by one sight
– Your beloved's face grown hard and aged, her beauty burned away
By acids . . . disappointment, contempt. Yet this must be so. Death
Precedes the rebirth. Life is a loop of exhaustion/renewal which can't
Be fast-forwarded, rewound or paused. Abide in God till grace returns,
The non-surgical facelift of humour restores youthfulness, the world
Quickens once more with significance and you want to play all
Your CDs at once but especially the Schubert Piano Trio in B flat,
Opus 99, where exuberance and tenderness uniquely combine
– So you put it on to speak for you of ardour, gratitude and love.

MY SECRET LIFE

Solitude on sunny mornings – nectar drunk from cups of gold.
And no TV next door. (Renee's out – though that's no guarantee.
She often leaves it blaring on – 'to keep the cats company'.)
So just the coffee-maker's mild huff and puff. Time to dream.
On a soft leather throne the philosopher-king. When I'm alone
Disappointment and shame disappear. What belongs to the world
May be dismissed with the world. But not withdrawn, madly *engagé*,
I spring up to seize a book, heft, riffle, sniff, the spine snug in a palm
As the thumb cuts and flips, riches fall open readily, the nose dips
To fragrance as heady as that of a naked saint's skin and the eyes feast
On lines that restore . . . strong and pure . . . just the same as at sixteen,
The *same* . . . my surreptitious exaltation, my clandestine happiness.

THE RAPTURE OF DUST

Don't lay me in earth. I've always loathed not just the concept
Of holy ground (a third of that unholy trinity – soil, faith and blood)
But the physical stuff itself – clay, clabber, mud and muck,
Heavy, sour, clinging, dark. Also, you get eaten by maggots.
Death should not deliver me to, but emancipate me from earth
In a final burst of incandescence – not to rot, dinner for insects,
But to blaze and be liberated into air, free from responsibility
And the shame of the sweating self, not to be circumscribed
Nor even detectable . . . either halfway to distant stars . . . or lodged
In your throat (for eavesdropping at source) – though more likely
In between, whirled round the globe. To soar above – or infiltrate
– But never to serve. Eternal the freedom and rapture of dust.